National Library
of Canada

Bibliothèque nationale
du Canada

D1298811

Bibliographic Style Manual

by
Danielle Thibault

Ottawa
1990

2-35136

Canadian Cataloguing in Publication Data
Thibault, Danielle
  Bibliographic style manual

Includes bibliographical references.
Issued also in French under title : Guide de
  rédaction bibliographique.
ISBN 0-660-13267-2
DSS Cat. no. SN3-247/1989E

1. Bibliographical citations--Handbooks, manuals,
etc. 2. Descriptive cataloguing--Handbooks, manuals,
etc. I. National Library of Canada II. Title.

Z1001.T4413 1990   010'.44   C90-090082-2

The paper used in this publication meets the minimum
requirements of American National Standard for Information Sciences — Permanence of Paper for Printed Library
Materials, ANSI Z39.48-1984.

©Minister of Supply and Services Canada 1989

Available in Canada through

Associated Bookstores
and other booksellers

or by mail from

Canadian Government Publishing Centre
Supply and Services Canada
Ottawa, Canada K1A 0S9

Catalogue No. SN3-247/1989E
ISBN 0-660-13267-2

Foreword

The *Bibliographic Style Manual* is an invaluable tool for bibliographers, librarians, researchers and writers. It is a practical guide that uses concrete examples to illustrate solutions to the problems of bibliographic presentation for most documents requiring bibliographic description.

In carrying out this project, which was begun a number of years ago, the editorial committee responsible for the manual's preparation placed great emphasis on uniformity, so as to make the bibliographic entries more understandable. The project was realized thanks to the steadfast effort of National Library of Canada staff members and the bibliographic experts who supported them.

With this first edition of the *Bibliographic Style Manual*, the National Library of Canada provides yet another means of making information and documentation more accessible.

Marianne Scott
National Librarian

Table of Contents

Part Two

LIST OF ILLUSTRATIONS

Introduction

This manual establishes the stylistic conventions for bibliographic entries. The principles and examples on the following pages make it possible to create a record for any document, or work, likely to be cited in a bibliography.

The Entry

A bibliographic entry may be defined as a standard set of data taken from a cited work. The purpose of this data is to provide as accurate a description as possible of the work so that it may be identified and located. Information about the document should, therefore, be recorded in accordance with formal rules. It should also be presented in a standard order, regardless of document type, so that the entry can be understood quickly and correctly, even if it is in a language that is unfamiliar to users of the bibliography.

The conventions in this manual are designed to ensure accurate, uniform and easy-to-understand descriptions of all types of documents that may be listed in a bibliography. Three components contribute to the accuracy, uniformity and clarity of bibliographic entries: the outline, which is applicable to all document types; technical punctuation, which clearly identifies each bibliographic element; and recording rules, which should make it possible to solve most problems encountered in recording information.

Outline

The outline of a bibliographic entry is taken from ISO Standard 690, *Documentation, bibliographic references: content, form and structure.*[*] It lists the elements required to describe one or more document types, including parts of documents, and establishes the order in which they are recorded. It will not always be necessary to use all the elements listed in the outline. The particular nature of the document to be cited and the needs of

---

* See Bibliography.

1

the bibliography's users will determine which of the elements should be included. However, the elements should always appear in the same order so as to provide uniformity in bibliographic entries and make it possible to consult an entry without knowing the language in which it was created.

Punctuation

Bibliographic entries use a technical form of punctuation, based on that in *ISBD (G): General international standard bibliographic description.*[*] It serves to identify clearly the fields of an entry and the elements within each field. Like the outline, this technical punctuation enhances the clarity of bibliographic entries by making it easier to identify items of bibliographic information.

Recording Rules

The recording rules are derived from current bibliographic practices and *Anglo-American cataloging rules*, the National Library of Canada's *Rules for interpreting the Anglo-American cataloguing rules*. These rules, which have been unified, codified and simplified at various times, ensure that bibliographic information is recorded with maximum accuracy.

The outline, the technical punctuation and the recording rules are also designed for easy use in computerized systems. The division into fields and the formal punctuation system are highly compatible with such systems.

The Manual

The manual is divided into two parts. Part One sets out the general conventions for creating entries for all document types. Part Two lists the elements that must be recorded for various formats and special types of documents, and discusses the particular features of these elements.

Part One

Part One consists of three chapters.

Chapter 1 gives the outline of an entry, explains the principles of bibliographic punctuation, and establishes conventions for recording information that is added, omitted or presumed by the compiler, and for noting errors that appear in the bibliographic information in the document.

---

* *See Bibliography.*

Chapter 2 specifies the conventions for each field. The field is defined, the punctuation required for each element in the field is described, and the recording rules for each element are established.

Chapter 3 explains the conventions for capitalization, abbreviation, translation and romanization.

Part Two

Part Two also contains three chapters.

Chapter 4 lists the conventions for the bibliographic description of various document formats, which are divided into the following categories:

Books, book parts and pamphlets
Braille and large-print documents
Machine-readable files (software)
Manuscripts
Maps and atlases
Microformos
Motion pictures and video recordings
Multimedia kits
Photographs
Printed music
Serials and serial parts
Slides and filmstrips
Sound recordings
Works of art

These document formats are presented in alphabetical order to facilitate consultation of the manual. The bibliographic information for each format is arranged in a standard order under four headings. At the beginning of each section is an outline of all the fields and elements required in an entry for the format in question; following the outline is a sample entry. (Note that not all the elements listed may appear in the sample entry.) Each section defines the document format (under "Purpose"); describes what part of the document should be consulted to obtain data for the entry ("Main Source of Information"); explains the changes required to adapt the general conventions in Part One to particular formats ("Special Features"); and presents general and particular examples of bibliographic entries. Some sections contain fifth and sixth headings under which are included the rules for document parts (e.g., a part of a book or an article in a periodical).

Chapter 5, entitled "Special Types of Documents", explains the rules for documents that pose special problems, such as how to create an author field for legislative documents, legal documents or conference proceedings. This chapter covers the following types of documents:

Conference proceedings
Government documents
Legal documents
Legislative documents
Patent documents
Standards
Theses

The sections are in alphabetical order, and the information is arranged as in the previous chapter, except that no outlines are included.

Chapter 6 is on bilingual documents. They are discussed in a separate chapter because the rules are general and applicable to all document types.

PART ONE

CHAPTER 1
General Conventions of Bibliographic Entries

Section 1
Outline

Purpose of a Bibliographic Entry

The purpose of a bibliographic entry is to describe a particular document as accurately as possible. The information in the entry should, therefore, be consistent with the information that appears in the source from which it is taken. It may, however, be adapted if necessary. In fact, if certain elements of information do not appear in the document, they may be taken from another source or may be presumed by the compiler. Such elements should be enclosed in brackets or explained in a note at the end of the entry.

Purpose of the Entry Outline

The outline is designed to ensure uniformity in the creation of entries so that all entries, for materials as diverse as books, periodicals and motion pictures, contain the same type of bibliographic information, arranged in the same order.

The outline lists the various items of bibliographic information, or "bibliographic elements". These elements are arranged in fields, each of which describes a particular feature of the document. The order of the various fields and the elements within them are modelled on ISO Standard 690.[*] The rules for recording each bibliographic element are given in Chapter 2.

---

[*] *See Bibliography.*

Description of the Entry Outline

3

The outline contains eleven fields, as follows:

1. Author

The author field records the name of the person or corporate body responsible for the document's intellectual or artistic content. Up to three persons or corporate bodies may be cited, provided that they share equal responsibility for creating the document and that the nature of this responsibility is identical.

If the nature of the responsibility differs, as in the case of an author and an illustrator, the author field should contain only the name of the person or corporate body primarily responsible for creating the document's intellectual or artistic content. Any other name should appear in the secondary author field.

Should the document have more than three authors, the name of the first or principal author is recorded in this field, followed by the Latin expression "et al.", which means "and others". Note that the author field rarely lists more than one corporate body because of the very restrictive rules for recording corporate names in this field (see Rule 27 - "Corporate Body as Author").

2. Title

The title field records the title, alternative title, a descriptive identifier (description of the general nature of the document), subtitle and parallel title. A bibliographic entry may contain some or all of these elements, depending on the information that appears in the document cited.

The descriptive identifier is included only if use of the document requires some specific technical equipment (e.g., for a motion picture or a sound disc) or if the user should possess some specialized knowledge (e.g., an understanding of Braille or the musical notation system).

3. Secondary Author

The secondary author field contains the names of persons and corporate bodies who performed a subsidiary function in the creation of the document (e.g., an illustrator, translator or preface writer) or coordinated production activities (e.g., the producer of a motion picture or the editor of a series of works).

4. Edition

Edition information usually consists of the edition number, sometimes followed by a word or expression that indicates the nature of the changes made to the previous edition or editions of the document (e.g., revised and enlarged). The edition field may also cite a person who played a major role in editing the document.

5. Issue Designation

The issue designation field is used only in bibliographic entries for serial publications (e.g., newspapers, periodicals and annual reports). It contains the volume number, issue number and date.

6. Publication Data

Publication data consists of three elements which are presented in a standard order: the place of publication, the publisher's name and the publication date.

7. Extent

The extent field gives the number of physical units contained in the document (e.g., the number of pages in a book or the number of reels in a motion picture). It may include technical information (e.g., the size of a motion picture, such as 16 mm) to help identify the type of equipment required to consult the document.

8. Series

The series field records the title of the series to which the document belongs and the number of the document within the series.

9. Notes

The notes are additional items of useful information (e.g., a publisher's production number) that cannot be recorded in any other field. Notes are optional and should be used sparingly so that entries do not become unnecessarily long.

No. FIELD	ELEMENTS
1. Author	Name of person or corporate body
2. Title	Title, alternative title, descriptive identifier, subtitle, parallel title
3. Secondary Authors	Name of preface writer, translator, illustrator, editor, producer, performer
4. Edition	Number, descriptor
5. Issue Designation	Volume, number, date
6. Publication Data	Place, publisher, date
7. Extent	Number of pages, volumes, discs, microfiches, etc.
8. Series	Title and numbering
9. Notes	Additional information
10. Standard Number	ISBN and ISSN
11. Location of a Part in Host Document	Page numbers, slide number, etc.

10. Standard Number

The standard number field contains the International Standard Book Number or International Standard Serial Number. The number is preceded by the acronym ISBN or ISSN.

11. Location in Host Document

Used only in a bibliographic entry that refers to part of a document, the location in host document indicates where the cited part is found in the document. This information may be a set of page numbers, a slide number or a microfilm reel number.

As can be seen, the general outline for an entry includes all the elements required to describe any document. However, an entry almost never contains all these elements. The particular nature of the document will determine which elements should be recorded. For instance, a book entry will omit fields 5 and 11, whereas an entry for a periodical will leave out fields 1, 8 and 11.

The bibliographic elements required in entries for specific types of documents are discussed in Part Two of this manual.

BOOK ENTRY OUTLINE   *Illustration no. 2*

No. FIELD	ELEMENTS
1. Author	Name of person or corporate body
2. Title	Title, alternative title, subtitle, parallel title
3. Secondary Authors	Name of preface writer, translator, illustrator, editor
4. Edition	Number, descriptor
6. Publication Data	Place, publisher, date
7. Extent	Number of pages, volumes
8. Series	Title and numbering
9. Notes	Additional information
10. Standard Number	ISBN

PERIODICAL ENTRY OUTLINE   *Illustration no. 3*

No. FIELD	ELEMENTS
2. Title	Title, alternative title, subtitle, parallel title
3. Secondary Author	Name of sponsoring body
4. Edition	Number, descriptor
5. Issue Designation	Volume, number, date
6. Publication Data	Place, publisher, date
7. Extent	Number of volumes
9. Notes	Additional information
10. Standard Number	ISSN

No. FIELD	ELEMENTS
1. Author	Name of personal or corporate author of chapter or section
2. Title	Title, alternative title, subtitle, parallel title of chapter or section
2. Title	Title, alternative title, subtitle, parallel title of book
3. Secondary Author	Name of preface writer, translator, illustrator, editor
4. Edition	Number, descriptor
6. Publication Data	Place, publisher, date
8. Series	Title and numbering
9. Notes	Additional information
10. Standard number	ISBN
11. Location in Book	Page numbers of the part

Part of a Document

The bibliographic elements given in the general entry outline may also be used to describe part of a document. A "part" is a designated unit within a larger document (e.g., a chapter or section of a book, an article in a periodical or a track on a sound disc).

The entry format is similar to that for a complete document, except that it contains two title fields (the title of the part and the title of the host document), which are distinguished by punctuation (see Chapter 1, Section 2). Note that an entry for part of a documentshould provide all the information necessary for locating both the document and the document part. Information on creating entries for parts of specific types of documents is given in Part Two of the manual.

BOOK ABBREVIATED ENTRY OUTLINE   *Illustration no. 5*

No. FIELD	ELEMENTS
1. Author	Name of person or corporate body
2. Title	Title, alternative title, subtitle, parallel title
4. Edition	Number, descriptor
6. Publication Data	Place, publisher, date
10. Standard Number	ISBN

PERIODICAL ABBREVIATED ENTRY OUTLINE   *Illustration no. 6*

No. FIELD	ELEMENTS
2. Title	Title, alternative title, subtitle, parallel title
3. Secondary Author	Name of sponsoring body
4. Edition	Number, descriptor
5. Issue Designation	Volume, number, date
6. Publication Data	Place, publisher, date
10. Standard Number	ISSN

Abbreviated Entry

A bibliography need not always provide the detailed entries outlined in the preceding tables. It may sometimes consist of entries that contain only the information indispensable for identifying the document. Nevertheless, an abbreviated entry should supply enough information for the user to understand the reference accurately and should, of course, present the elements in the standard order. Abbreviated entries may, for example, include the elements in Illustration no. 5.

5

Section 2
Punctuation

Purpose of Bibliographic Punctuation

6 The technical punctuation system described here is taken from the *General international standard bibliographic description.*[*] Technical punctuation, as opposed to grammatical punctuation, is used to identify bibliographic elements and fields. Like the standard order of the elements, this punctuation system helps to create uniformity in bibliographic entries and to make the information accessible to users who may not be familiar with the language of the entry. Note that bibliographic punctuation is sometimes used in addition to grammatical punctuation. For instance, if a title ends with an exclamation point or question mark, the prescribed colon nevertheless precedes the subtitle (see Rule 58).

> What! : another minimum wage study?
> What became of Angelo? : the life of Pope John XXIII

The particular applications of bibliographic punctuation are discussed in the rules for each field. However, a few general conventions are given below, along with a table of bibliographic punctuation marks.

Punctuation between Fields

7 Except for the last element in the entry, the final element of each field is followed by a period, space, en dash and another space. If this element is an abbreviation containing a period (e.g., "ed.") or ellipsis points without brackets, no period is added.

> Gordon, Walter J. – What is happening to Canada

and not

> Gordon, Walter J.. – What is happening to Canada

---

* See Bibliography.

> 3rd ed. – Toronto : Oxford University Press

and not

> 3rd ed.. – Toronto : Oxford University Press
>
> Klein, A.M. – Hath not a Jew . . . –

and not

> Klein, A.M.. – Hath not a Jew . . . –

If the en dash cannot be produced by the equipment available, it may be replaced by two successive hyphens.

> Gordon, Walter J. -- What is happening to Canada
>
> 3rd ed. -- Toronto : Oxford University Press

Spacing

All prescribed punctuation marks or typographical symbols are preceded and followed by a space.

8

Exceptions to this rule are **the comma, the hyphen, the slash, the full stop, parentheses, angle quotes and square brackets**. No space precedes the comma, the hyphen, the slash, the full stop, the closing parenthesis, angle quote and square bracket. No space follows the hyphen, the slash, the opening parenthesis, angle quote and square bracket. The comma and the full stop are followed by a space. However, it is possible for the hyphen to be followed by four spaces, a situation occurring solely in the case of a document that is still being published (e.g., a periodical). See Illustration no. 7 on the following page.

Illustration no. 7   *PUNCTUATION AND SPACING*

Field	Punctuation Mark	Function
(The symbol "▮" is not a bibliographic punctuation mark and is used here only to represent a space.)		
All except last	.▮–▮	Ends field
Author	▮;▮	Separates author names
Title		
- of part of		
document	« »	Encloses title of part of a document
- of document	[ ]	Encloses descriptive identifier
	▮:▮	Precedes subtitle
	▮=▮	Precedes parallel title
	.▮	Precedes supplement title
Secondary Author	,▮	Separates names of subsidiary authors
Edition	n/a	No technical punctuation
Issue		
Designation	,▮	Separates number elements
	( )	Encloses date
	/	Separates consecutive numbers or dates
	-	Separates consecutive sequences of numbers or dates
	-▮▮▮▮	Indicates that document is still being published
	▮;▮	Separates non-consecutive sequences of numbers or dates
	▮:▮	Precedes name of publisher and separates names of co-publishers in the same location.
Publication Data	▮;▮	Precedes second place of publication
	,▮	Precedes date of publication
	-	Separates dates of publication of document published in several parts over several years
	-▮▮▮▮	Indicates that document in several parts is still being published
Extent	,▮	Separates elements
Series	( )	Encloses series information
	▮;▮	Precedes numbering of document within series
	.▮	Separates series from subseries information
Notes	.▮–▮	Separates notes
Standard Number	,▮	Separates standard numbers
Location in	n/a	No technical punctuation
host document		

Section 3
Additions, Omissions, Assumptions and Errors

Additions

An "addition" is an element of information added to a bibliographic entry by the compiler. There are two types of additions: those taken from the document and those obtained from other sources (e.g., standard reference works or publishers' catalogues).

9

Additions Taken from Document

This type of addition consists of information not usually found in an entry. It is enclosed in parentheses and serves to clarify other bibliographic elements or establish the identity of a document that could be mistaken for another. Such additions are used sparingly.

10

> Markham (Ont.) : Penguin Books, 1981

In this example, the province was added because the place of publication is not a major city.

> Echo (Belleville, Ont.)
>
> Echo (Swan Lake, Man.)

In these examples, adding the names of towns and provinces enables the user of the bibliography to distinguish between the two newspapers.

Additions Obtained from Other Sources

The second type of addition consists of elements that normally appear in an entry but originate from a source other than the cited document. These elements are enclosed in brackets.

11

> [Ottawa] : Oberon Press, 1972

In this example, the place of publication was not indicated in the document and so was taken from another source. If a field contains two related bibliographic elements taken from a source other than the document, they are enclosed in one set of brackets.

[Medicine Hat, Alta. : G. Newton], 1984

Omissions

12

Some elements of information, (e.g., parts of very long titles), may be deliberately omitted from a bibliography. Such omissions are indicated by ellipsis points in brackets. There should be a space before and after each period of the ellipsis.

As an example, the title

Statement respecting the Earl of Selkirk's settlement upon the Red River in North America; its destruction in 1815 and 1816; and the messacre of Governor Semple and his party. With observations upon a recent publication, entitled "A narrative of occurrences in the Indian countries," &c.

could be shortened in the entry as

Statement respecting the Earl of Selkirk's settlement [...] in North America; its destruction [...] and the massacre of Governor Semple and his party [...] &c.

If an omission occurs at the end of the title field, the closing bracket is followed immediately by a period.

The one hundred prize questions in Canadian history and the answers of "Hermes" [...].

If an ellipsis is contained in the original title, it should, of course, not be enclosed in brackets in the entry.

... I am prepared to die

I am ... a cloud

Hath not a Jew ...

In the last example, no period is added after the ellipsis to close the field (see Rule 7 - "Punctuation between Fields").

The convention for omission is not used to indicate the absence of bibliographic elements or fields that do not apply to a given document; nor is it used in abbreviated entries.

Assumptions

13

If an added element of information is uncertain, it should be followed by a question mark. Both the element and the question mark are enclosed in brackets, as are any additions taken from a source other than the document in question (see Rule 11).

> Perth (Ont.): Wellspring Press, [1985?]

In the example above, the publication date was determined by conjecture based on various other sources. The date is followed by a question mark and enclosed in brackets because there is no way of confirming that the document was actually published that year.

Errors

Incorrect forms appearing in the document should be enclosed in brackets or followed by the Latin expression "sic", meaning "thus".

14

> Words in th[e] fire
>
> Siddall, Elizabeth. – Poems of Elizabeth Siddal [sic]
>
> "Stages in the last delaciation [sic] of northern Canada"

In the above examples, the titles were recorded as they appear in the original documents. The brackets and term "sic" indicate what are probably typographical errors.

CHAPTER 2
Fields and Elements of an Entry

Section 1
Author

Definition of Author

The "author" is the person or corporate body primarily responsible for the intellectual or artistic content of a work. It may, for example, be a person who wrote a book or a periodical article, compiled a bibliography, took a photograph, composed a piece of music, designed a software program, created a work of art or drew a map.

15

Punctuation

If the author field contains two or three authors' names, they are separated by a semicolon, preceded and followed by a space (;).
The field is closed by a period, space, en dash and another space.

16

Personal Author

Recording Rules

The main purpose of the following rules is to ensure the accurate identification of authors, even when variants of names appear on the documents. For instance, if one entry records the author's surname and initial, and another entry lists the author's surname and forename, the user might erroneously believe there are two different authors.

17

The author's name is recorded as given in the document's main source of information. The surname is entered before the forename or initial.

The "main source of information" is the part of the document from which information is taken for the bibliographic entry (e.g., the title page of a book or the record label). The main sources of information for each type of document are named in Part Two of this manual.

> Gundy, H. Pearson
> Hesse, M.G.

MacDonald, Flora
Macdonald, J.D.
Ouellet, Jean
Ouellette, Fernand

The author field may contain no surname if the author is a pope, monarch, emperor, cleric or saint.

Paul VI
André, Frère

Name with One or More Initials

18   If the name in the main source of information could be confused with another author's name, the entry should provide the detail necessary to avoid any ambiguity. For instance,

Jones, D.L.

could be recorded in the entry as

Jones, D[avid] L.

The part of the name that does not appear in the main source of information is enclosed in brackets.

Name with More than One Form within Document

19   When the author's name appears in more than one form in the document, the entry should follow the form given in the main source of information. For example,

Fennario, David

and not

Wiper, David

Name with More than One Form in Various Documents

20   If a bibliography lists more than one document by the same author, but the form of the author's name varies from one document to another, one form of the name should be selected and used consistently in all entries. For instance, a choice must be made between

Des Rochers, Alfred

and

DesRochers, Alfred

and

Desrochers, Alfred

Prefixed Name

When the author's surname contains a prefix, the entry is made under the prefix, unless usage dictates otherwise. Capitalization of the prefix also depends on usage, which can generally be ascertained from the main source of information. If the author's name appears in block capitals in the main source of information, the correct capitalization should be determined from other parts of the document (e.g., the book cover or record sleeve).

21

> De Konnick, Charles
> De l'île, Claude
> De la Roche, Mazo
> de Veauce, C. de Cadier
> Du Berger, Pierre

but

> Champlain, Samuel de
> Granmont, Monique de

Cross-references should be provided to direct the user to the correct form of the author's name.

> l'île, Claude De   **SEE**   De l'île, Claude
> de Champlain, Samuel   **SEE**   Champlain, Samuel de

Compound Surname

There are two types of compound surnames — hyphenated and nonhyphenated. Both types are recorded as the first element in the author field.

22

> Jones-Davies, Louise
> Lloyd-Jones, David
> Chapdelaine Gagnon, Jean

Cross-references may be provided to direct users to the correct form of the author's name.

> Davies, Louise Jones-   **SEE** Jones-Davies, Louise
> Gagnon, Jean Chapdelaine   **SEE** Chapdelaine Gagnon, Jean

Title of Address, Profession, Nobility, Office or Religion

A title or rank is recorded in the entry if it appears in the main source of information and meets one of the following conditions:

23

1) It is an indispensable element of identification:

> Smith, John B., Mrs.

2) Its omission leaves only the author's surname or forename:

> Marie-Victorin, Frère
>
> Smyth, Dr.

3) It is commonly associated with the author's name:

> Osler, William, Sir
>
> George, Dan, Chief

4) It is required to distinguish the author from another author with a similar or identical name:

> Groulx, Lionel, abbé
>
> Groulx, Lionel

Pseudonym

24

If the only author name that appears in the document's main source of information is a pseudonym, it should be recorded in the author field of the bibliographic entry.

If the bibliography lists documents under the author's real name and documents under the pseudonym, the names should be cross-referenced.

> Skelton, Robin **SEE ALSO** Zuk, Georges
>
> Zuk, Georges **SEE ALSO** Skelton, Robin

Author Unknown

25

When the name of the author is not known, the bibliographic entry is recorded under the title of the document.

Corporate Author

Definition

26

A corporate body is an organization or a group of persons identified by a particular name and acting as a single entity. For bibliographic purposes, corporate bodies also include conferences, symposiums and other events whose proceedings are published. Listed below are several types of corporate bodies:

Private corporate bodies, e.g., associations, foundations, business firms, non-profit organizations, conferences, meetings, exhibitions, political parties, and fairs:

> Atlantic Queen Crab Association
>
> Canadian Federation of Independent Business
>
> Canadian Hunger Foundation
>
> Canadian Standards Association

    Colloque Augustin-Frigon
    Liberal Party of Ontario
    Man in Motion World Tour
    National Book Festival

Governments, e.g., national, provincial, regional or civic:

    Canada

    Manitoba

    Montréal

    Vancouver

Public corporate bodies, whether legal entities or parts of legal entities, e.g., educational institutions, courts, crown corporations, government departments, and heads of state or government:

    Brock University

    Canada Mortgage and Housing Corporation

    Canada. Department of National Health and Welfare

    Canada. Prime Minister

    New Brunswick. Department of Fisheries and Environment

Religious bodies, e.g., churches, dioceses, religious groups or orders, and religious dignitaries:

    Catholic Church

    United Church of Canada

    Jesuits

    Ursulines

International organizations:

    United Nations

    Unesco

    International Civil Aviation Organization

Corporate Body as Author

A corporate body is considered to be the author of a document if the document meets one of the following conditions:

27

1)   It is administrative in nature, e.g., a policy manual, financial activities report, personnel or members' directory, or resources inventory:

    Concordia University. Arts and Sciences Special Task Force on Curriculum. – Report

2) It reflects the collective thought of the group, e.g., a brief:

> Association of Canadian Publishers. – Children's book publishing in Canada : a brief
>
> Progress Canada West. – Canadian environmental concerns : progress report

3) It is legal in nature, e.g., a bill or regulation:

> Nova Scotia. – Trade union act : Statutes of Nova Scotia, ch. 19, proclaimed October 1, 1972

4) The document reflects the collective activity of the group, e.g., conference proceedings, expedition results or exhibition catalogues;

> National Rail Passenger Conference (1st, 1976, Regina). – Proceedings of the 1st National Rail Passenger Conference, Regina, Saskatchewan, Canada, October 29-31, 1976
>
> National Gallery of Canada. – Sculpture '67

5) It is a map that is a product of the corporate body's collective activity:

> Canadian Automobile Association. CAA Ottawa. – The Regional Municipality of Ottawa-Carleton : 1988 regional road system

6) It is a sound recording of popular musical works by various composers, in which case the performing group is cited in the author field:

> Canadian Brass. – Christmas with the Canadian Brass

When none of the above conditions apply, the entry should be recorded under the name of the personal author if this name appears in the main source of information; otherwise, it should be recorded under the title (see Rule 37 - "Document Produced by an Individual for a Corporate Body").

Recording Rules

28

Corporate names are recorded as they appear in the main source of information. Unlike personal names, they are not inverted in bibliographic entries. Articles preceding corporate names are omitted.

> Children's Aid Society of British Columbia

For the conventions governing the capitalization of corporate names, see Rule 133.

Corporate Author with Subordinate Levels

29

When a corporate author is part of a larger corporate body (e.g., a university faculty or government department), the author field should list the name of the parent corporate body before the author name so that the document may be clearly identified. The two names are separated by a period and a space. Only the elements of the hierarchy which are necessary to avoid ambiguity are recorded.

> Brock University. Faculty Association

Canadian Bar Association. Committee on the Reform of Parliament

Ontario. Workers' Compensation Board

Corporate Name in Several Languages

If the document's main source of information gives the corporate name in more than one language, the author field should cite the name in the language of the document title. For bilingual documents, however, the corporate author name is recorded in the language of the bibliography's intended users. For instance, if the document gives the corporate name in English and French, and the bibliography is intended for Francophone users, the French name of the corporate body is listed in the author field.

30

Name with More than One Form within the Document

If more than one version of the corporate name appears in the document, the entry should record the name found in the main source of information. For example, if the name on the title page is "Department of Transport", the author field should contain

31

Canada. Department of Transport

rather than

Canada. Transport Canada

Name with More than One Form in Various Documents

If a bibliography lists more than one document by the same corporate author, but the form of the corporate name varies from one document to another, the most recent form of the corporate name (which can be determined from publication dates) should be selected and used consistently. For example, the author name would be listed as

32

Canadian Association of Occupational Therapists

and not

Canadian Association of Occupational Therapy

Unused forms of the corporate name should be cross-referenced with the form used in the entry.

Canadian Association of Occupational Therapy

SEE

Canadian Association of Occupational Therapists

Change of Corporate Name

33

When a corporate body has changed its name, the new name is used in the entry if it appears in the document cited.

In the example below, the corporate body has changed its name several times since the body was established.

> Canada. Department of Citizenship and Immigration
> (from 1950 to 1966)
>
> Canada. Department of Manpower and Immigration
> (from 1967 to 1977)
>
> Canada. Employment and Immigration Canada
> (since 1977)

Therefore, for all documents published by this corporate body from 1950 to 1966, the first form of the name appears in any bibliographic entry; for all documents published between 1967 and 1977, the second form of the name is recorded; and for all documents published since 1977, the third form of the corporate name is used.

All versions of the name that appear in the bibliography are cross-referenced. For example,

> Canada. Department of Citizenship and Immigration
> **SEE ALSO**
> Canada. Department of Manpower and Immigration

Corporate Body Identified by an Initialism

34

Even if a corporate body is also known by an initialism, its full corporate name should be cited in entries in order to avoid ambiguity.

> Canadian Union of Public Employees

instead of

> CUPE

The initialism should be cross-referenced with the full form of the corporate name.

> CUPE
> **SEE**
> Canadian Union of Public Employees

Corporate Body Identified by an Acronym

35

If a corporate body is identified by an acronym (an initialism that is pronounced like a word; e.g., Unesco), the acronym is used in the author field.

Unesco

rather than

United Nations Educational, Scientific and Cultural Organization

The full form of the corporate name may be cross-referenced with the acronym.

United Nations Educational, Scientific and Cultural Organization

SEE

Unesco

Addition to Corporate Author Name

If the corporate name listed in the main source of information could be confused with another, the author field should provide sufficient additional information to identify the author clearly. Additional information, usually taken from the document, is inserted in parentheses (see Rule 10). Some common additions to corporate author entries include the geographic jurisdiction in which the corporate body operates, the location of its head office and the institution with which it is affiliated.

36

Trinity College (Cobourg, Ont.)
Trinity College (Hartford, Conn.)

Conferences, seminars or meetings bearing the same name are clearly identified by the addition of the following elements:
- an ordinal number if the event is part of an annual series;
- the year; and
- the location of the event.

These items of information are enclosed in parentheses and separated by commas.

Symposium on Exact Philosophy (1st, 1971, Montréal)

Document Produced by an Individual for a Corporate Body

If an individual working as an employee or in some other capacity for a corporate body produces a document that meets one of the requirements of Rule 27 (i.e., it is administrative or legal in nature, reflects the collective thought or activity of the group, or reports on corporate resources), the name of the corporate body is recorded in the author field. The secondary author field should contain the name of the personal author and a description of the personal author's role, as described in the main source of information.

37

University of Waterloo. – Women's studies handbook : a guide to relevant research at the University of Waterloo. – Compiled by Lindsay Dorney

Note that when the corporate body is acting only as the publisher of the document, its name is recorded only in the publication data field.

Joint Authorship

For bibliographic purposes, there are three types of documents produced by joint authorship:
- new documents to which various authors contributed (e.g., a musical work created by a composer and a songwriter);
- previously published documents that have been modified (e.g., a novel adapted for film);
- documents in several parts by various authors (e.g., an anthology), which may or may not be grouped under a general title.

New Documents

Two or Three Authors

38

For a document produced by two or three authors, the names are listed in the author field in the same order as given in the main source of information and are separated by semicolons.

> Hébert, Jacques ; Trudeau, Pierre Elliott
>
> Argue, Robert ; Emanuel, Barbara ; Graham, Stephen

However, if one name is more prominently presented in the main source of information (e.g., appears in larger type), it is recorded first in the bibliographic entry.

Authors with Same Surname

39

For a document produced by two authors with the same surname, each author's name is recorded in full and in the same order in which it appears in the main source of information.

> Foster, John ; Foster, Janet

Four or More Authors

40

For a document with more than three authors, the author field cites the full name of the first author, followed by the expression "et al." (from the Latin "et alii", which means "and others").

> Wolfe, J.S. et al. – Farm family financial crisis : overview of impacts and responses

Writer and Artist

If a writer and an artist have collaborated on a document (e.g., a comic strip), the first name that appears in the main source of information should be recorded in the author field. The name of the second person is entered in the secondary author field.

41

> Wynne-Jones, Tim. – Architect of the moon. – Pictures by Ian Wallace

However, if the name of the second author is presented more prominently (e.g., in larger type) in the main source of information, that name is the one that should appear in the author field.

Illustrator

As an illustrator's role is subsidiary, illustrators are never cited in the author field but, rather, in the secondary author field.

42

> Collard, Edgar Andrew. – Stories about 125 years at Touche, Ross. – Illustrations by Irma Coucill

Composer and Songwriter

For a musical work with lyrics, the composer's name should appear in the author field, and the songwriter's name should be listed in the secondary author field.

43

> Campbell, Norman. – Bosom friends [music]. – Words by Donald Harron

Interviewer and Interviewee

If the document is the record of an interview presented in a question-and-answer format, the name of the interviewee appears in the author field, and the name of the interviewer is recorded in the secondary author field.

44

> Gould, Glenn. – Conversations with Glenn Gould. – Introduction and interviews by Jonathan Cott

However, if the interviewer summarizes or reformulates the words of the interviewee, the interviewer's name is the one that should appear in the author field.

> Fischler, Stan. – Those were the days : the lore of hockey by the legends of the game

The document in this example consists of a collection of essays by Stan Fischler, most of which are edited summaries of his interviews with former athletes.

Collective Author

When a document has several authors grouped under a single collective name, the author field records the collective name.

45

> Company of Artists and Patrons. – Portfolio '83

Previously Published Documents

Adapted Works

46

When a work is adapted — that is, transposed to a different medium or form (e.g., a novel adapted for stage or film, or a musical work transcribed for different instruments) – the bibliographic entry is created under the adaptor's name, except for films and video recordings, which are always listed under their titles (see Rule 51 - "Motion Pictures and Video Recordings").

The original author and title of an adapted work are cited in a note if they are not named in the title field.

Annotated Works

47

For an annotated work, the name of the annotator appears in the author field if the commentary is longer than the original text.

> Wrenn, C.L. – Beowulf with the Finnesburg fragment

However, if the original text is longer than the commentary, the author field cites the original author, and the annotator's name appears in the secondary author field.

> Lampman, Archibald. – The story of an affinity. – Ed. D.M.R. Bentley

Translated Documents

48

Translators are never cited in the author field, but rather in the secondary author field.

> Roy, Gabrielle. – The tin flute. – Translated by Hannah Josephson

Edited, Revised, Corrected or Enlarged Documents

49

When a document has been edited, revised, corrected or enlarged by a person other than the original author, that person's name is recorded in the edition field. The original author is cited in the author field.

> Fowler, H.W. – Modern English Usage. – Revised by Ernest Gowers

Documents in Several Parts by Various Authors

Documents in several parts produced by different authors may be divided into two categories: those with and those without general titles.

Documents with General Titles

Documents in several parts with a general title include collections, motion pictures, video recordings and sound recordings.

Collections

The first field in an entry for a collection is always the title field, as the editor's role is to compile the contributions of the authors (e.g., in an anthology or conference proceedings). The editor's name is recorded in the secondary author field.

50

> An anthology of Canadian literature in English. – Edited by Russel Brown and Donna Bennett

Motion Pictures and Video Recordings

Entries for motion pictures and video recordings are always listed under their titles. As the producer's contribution is to coordinate production activities, the producer's name appears in the secondary author field.

51

> Bix [motion picture]. – Produced by Brigitte Berman

Sound Recordings

For sound recordings of works by different composers, the performer is cited in the author field. The works performed may be listed in a note.

52

> Boyd, Liona. – The best of Liona Boyd [sound recording]

Documents with No General Title

Collections

For an untitled collection of works by various authors, the first author and work are cited first, followed by the second author and work, and the third author and work. These elements are separated by the same punctuation used to close a field: a period, space, en dash and space.

53

> Wollstonecraft, Mary. – A vindication of the rights of women. – Mill, John Stuart. – The subjection of women

For untitled collections of more than three works, the first author and title are cited in the author and title fields, and the other authors and works are listed in a note. All works are cross-referenced with the first work if there is reason to believe that users may wish to consult them. When the name of the editor or compiler appears in the main source of information, it is recorded in the secondary author field.

Mill, John Stuart. – The subjection of women

SEE

Wollstonecraft, Mary. – A vindication of the rights of women. – Mill, John Stuart. – The subjection of women

Sound Recordings

54

There are different rules for classical music recordings and popular music recordings.

Classical Music

55

The rules for collections also apply to classical music recordings: the first composer and work are cited first, followed by the second composer and work, and the third composer and work. The performer is cited in the secondary author field. The elements are separated by the same punctuation used to close a field: a period, space, en dash and space.

Hindemith, Paul. – Sonata [sound recording]. – Dutilleux, Henri. – Sonate pour hautbois et piano. – Poulenc, Francis. – Sonate

All the works are cross-referenced with the first work if there is reason to believe that users may wish to consult them.

Poulenc, Francis. – Sonate.

SEE

Hindemith, Paul. – Sonata [sound recording]. – Dutilleux, Henri. – Sonate pour hautbois et piano. – Poulenc, Francis. – Sonate

Dutilleux, Henri. – Sonate pour hautbois et piano.

SEE

Hindemith, Paul. – Sonata [sound recording]. – Dutilleux, Henri. – Sonate pour hautbois et piano. – Poulenc, Francis. – Sonate

For an untitled recording of more than three works, the composer and title of the first work are cited at the beginning of the entry, and the other composers and works are listed in a note.

Popular Music

56

For a popular music recording with no general title, the entry is created under the name of the performer. If the recording consists of up to three works, the titles are listed in the title field. If there are more than three works, only the first title is cited in the title field, and the others may be listed in a note.

Section 2
Title

Definition

As the term or expression used to identify a document, the title generally makes it possible to distinguish the document from any other. The title usually appears in the main source of information, but may also appear on a book cover or jacket, a record sleeve or a video-recording container.

57

Punctuation

Angle quotes (« ») are used to enclose the title of part of a document.

Brackets ([ ]) have two functions: to enclose a descriptive identifier and to indicate a title supplied by the compiler for an untitled document.

A colon preceded and followed by a space (:) should appear before a subtitle.

An equals sign preceded and followed by a space (=) appears before a parallel title.

A period followed by a space (.) separates the title of a document from the title of a supplement.

The field is closed by a period, space, en dash and another space.

58

Recording Rules

General Conventions

Titles in the entry are usually recorded with the same spelling, word division and punctuation given in the main source of information. However, special conventions govern capitalization and romanization.

59

Spelling and Word Division

Any irregular spelling or word division given in the title should be maintained in the entry, since it is usually intended by the author or publisher as an intrinsic part of the title.

> Charlie Farquharson's jogfree of Canda : the whirld and other places
>
> How to write a be$t $eller
>
> Pnomes jukollages & other stunzas

However, if the title obviously contains a typographical error, it should be indicated by one of the conventions described in Rule 14 ("Errors").

Punctuation Present in Title

Any punctuation in the title as it appears in the main source of information should be recorded in the entry. Exclamation points, question marks, ellipses and quotation marks should be faithfully reproduced even if the result is double punctuation at the end of the title field (see Rule 6 - "Purpose of Bibliographic Punctuation").

> C.A.U.T. bulletin
>
> The RCMP
>
> 30 energy-efficient houses . . . you can build
>
> Why rock the boat?

Bibliographic punctuation is added to the literary punctuation to indicate the bibliographic elements. Note that there are no spaces between the letters of an acronym or initialism.

Capitalization

Capitalization of the title in the entry follows the conventions in Rules 135 to 139 unless consistently irregular usage in the document indicates an intentional deviation by the author or publisher.

> The "I AM" discourses
>
> artmagazine
>
> enRoute
>
> NeWest plays by women

Title in a Different Script

Titles appearing in a non-Latin alphabet are romanized according to the conventions in Chapter 3, Section 5 ("Romanization").

Alternative Title

Any alternative title should be included in the entry, as it is part of the title proper. In fact, a work is often better known by its alternative title. All punctuation in the alternative title is transcribed, and the first word is capitalized.

60

> Clemo, Ebenezer. – Canadian homes or The mystery solved
>
> Beckwith, Julia Catherine. – St. Ursula's Convent or The nun of Canada

Title with Author's Name

If the name of a personal or corporate author appears as an intrinsic part of the title in the main source of information, it is recorded in the title field, even if it is already listed in the author field.

61

> Pearson, Lester B. – Mike : The memoirs of the Right Honourable Lester B. Pearson
>
> Service, Robert. – Collected Poems of Robert Service

Title within Title

If the title contains the title of another work, the title of this second document is recorded in the title field with its punctuation.

62

> Frampton, Rhonda Heather. – An interpretation of Dante Gabriel Rossetti's "A last confession"

Different Versions of Title in Main Source of Information

When a title appears in more than one language in the chief source of information, each of these different versions of the title must be transcribed. Each one of these titles is preceded by an equals sign (=), preceded and followed by a space. These titles are called parallel titles. Parallel titles are found, among other places, in many Canadian official publications and in the publications of international organizations. To apply this rule, all these different versions of the title should appear in the same chief source of information (eg. on the title page of a book or the label of a sound recording. See Chapter 6, "Bilingual Documents".).

63

> Guide to federal electoral districts = Gide des circonscriptions électorales fédérales
>
> Bottin des femmes professionnelles et commerçantes = Career women on record
>
> Offenbach, Jacques. – Les contes d'Hoffmann [sound recording] = The tales of Hoffmann

Parallel titles are cross-referenced with the author name and document title if there is reason to believe that users may search for the document under its parallel title.

Guide des circonscriptions électorales fédérales

SEE

Guide to federal electoral districts = Guide des circonscriptions électorales fédérales

Career Women on Record

SEE

Bottin des femmes professionnelles et commerçantes = Career Women on Record

Offenbach, Jacques. – The tales of Hoffmann

SEE

Offenbach, Jacques. – Les contes d'Hoffmann [sound recording] = The tales of Hoffmann

Descriptive Identifier

64

A descriptive identifier is a term or expression recorded in the title field to indicate the format or medium of the document. It is listed only if special equipment (e.g., a tape player or slide projector) or specialized knowledge (e.g., of printed music or braille) is required to consult a document.

The descriptive identifier is inserted in brackets after the last word of the title or alternative title, and thus before any subtitle(s) or parallel title(s). It is always in lower case and in the singular.

Below is a sample list of descriptive identifiers:

filmstrip

microform

motion picture

multimedia kit

slide

sound recording

See Part Two of this manual for specific descriptive identifiers used with various document types.

Adams, Bryan. – Into the fire [sound recording]

Bach, Johann Sebastian. – Brandenburg concertos [sound recording] = Les concertos brandebourgeois = Brandenburgische Konzerte

Baker, Michael C. – The grey fox [sound recording] : original soundtrack

Mendes, John G. – An analysis of the application and structure of the right to equality in the Canadian Charter of Rights and Freedoms [microform]

Rabid [motion picture]

Ravel, Maurice. – Pavane pour une infante défunte [music]

If all the elements of a bibliography are in the same format or medium, or have been divided into like categories, the descriptive identifier need not appear in each entry. For instance, it would be redundant to indicate the descriptive identifier "sound recording" in every entry of a bibliography that lists only documents in that format.

Subtitle

A subtitle is a secondary title that appears under or after the main title in the document's main source of information. Subtitles are recorded in the bibliographic entry because they often help to identify or describe the work. They are separated from the title by a colon preceded and followed by a space, even if the title already ends with literary punctuation (e.g., a question mark or exclamation point). The same convention is used to separate two subtitles.

65

> Raising brighter children : a program for busy parents
>
> Antiques & art : the magazine for fine art collectors and investors
>
> A programmed instruction workbook : dangerous goods for air transport : the operator's responsibilities
>
> Immigrating to Canada : who is allowed? : what is required? : how to do it!
>
> If they do not appear in the main source of information, subtitles should be listed in a note.

Abridgement of Title

Titles are abridged, or abbreviated, in entries only if space for the bibliography is limited. Abridgement is generally not advisable because it could cause confusion for the user.

An abridged title or subtitle should not omit any essential information or become ambiguous. The first few words of the title must be retained, and omissions are indicated by an ellipsis enclosed in brackets: [...].

66

In the example below, the title

> Williams, W. – The traveller's and tourist's guide through the United States of America, Canada, etc. containing the routes of travel by railroad, steamboat, stage and canal; together with descriptions of, and routes to, the principal places of fashionable and healthful resort; with other valuable information; accompanied by an entirely new and authentic map of the United States, including California, Oregon, etc., and a map of the island of Cuba

is shortened to

> Williams, W. – The traveller's and tourist's guide through the United States [...], Canada, etc. containing [...] routes [...] by railroad, steamboat, stage and canal [...]

Periodical titles are abbreviated according to established standards: *American national standard for information sciences – abbreviation of titles of publications* (*ANSI Z39.5-1985*), by the American National Standards Institute, for periodicals in English, and

Documentation – Règles pour l'abréviation des mots dans les titres et des titres des publications (ISO 4-1984(F)), for works in French.[*]

A bibliography with abridged periodical titles should provide a key to the abbreviations used.

Untitled Document

67

If no title appears in the main source of information or elsewhere in the document, the entry should provide a brief descriptive title in brackets.

> Concordia University. Centre for Continuing Studies. –[Calendar]

Title of Document Part

68

The title and subtitle of part of a document should be recorded in the entry as it appears at the head of the document part; the table of contents should not be used as the main source of information, as it may list an abridged or modified version of the title. Capitalization follows the same conventions as for document titles (see Chapter 3, Section 1).

The title of a document part is enclosed in angle quotes (« »). There is no space between the opening quote and the first word nor between the closing quote and the last word or punctuation mark.

> «I80N/80 : the skin of the earth»
>
> «For Sue-Sue (Sue-Ad)»

When the mechanical means available to the compiler of the bibliography do not permit the reproduction of angle quotes (« »), quotation marks (" ") are used in their stead. Single quotation marks (' ') are used when double quotation marks are called for. Thus the titles

> «Zeno's paradox : Mallarmé, Valéry, and the Symbolist "movement"»
>
> «Mahler's "Todtenfeier" and the problem of program music»

are recorded as

> "Zeno's paradox : Mallarmé, Valéry, and the Symbolist 'movement'"
>
> "Mahler's 'Todtenfeier' and the problem of program music"

The double quotes that appear in the last example are part of the title.

---

[*] *See Bibliography.*

Document with Several Works under General Title

If a document containing several different works lists both a general title and the individual titles of the works in the main source of information, only the general title is recorded in the title field. The individual titles are shown in the notes field.

69

> NeWest plays by women. – Edited by Diane Bessai, Don Kerr. – Edmonton : NeWest Publishers, c1987. – 251 p. – (Prairie Play Series ; 7). – Contents: Play memory, by Joanna M. Glass; The occupation of Heather Rose, by Wendy Lill; Inside out, by Pamela Boyd; Whiskey six cadenza, by Sharon Pollock.

Untitled Document with Several Works

If a document containing two or three works by one or more authors has no general title, the title of each work is recorded after the name of its author, in the order given in the main source of information. Each bibliographic element (i.e., each author's name and each title) appears in a separate field, ending with a period, space, en dash and another space.

70

> Souster, Raymond. – The colour of the times. – Ten elephants on Yonge street

> Schafer, R. Murray. – Arcana [sound recording]. – East. – Psalm. – Miniwanka

All other works are cross-referenced with the first work listed in the entry, if there is reason to believe that users may wish to consult them.

> Souster, Raymond. – Ten elephants on Yonge street
>
> **SEE**
>
> Souster, Raymond. – The colour of the times. – Ten elephants on Yonge street

> Schafer, R. Murray. – East [sound recording]
>
> **SEE**
>
> Schafer, R. Murray. – Arcana [sound recording]. – East. – Psalm. – Miniwanka

For untitled collections of more than three works, the first author and title are cited in the author and title fields, and the other authors and works are listed in a note. All works are cross-referenced with the first work if there is reason to believe that users may wish to consult them. When the name of the editor or compiler appears in the main source of information, it is recorded in the secondary author field.

Document in Several Units under General Title Only

If the work is one of several units in a larger document and has no individual title, it is recorded under the general title of the document and identified by its volume number. Arabic numerals are used, even if the work has Roman numerals, and are separated from the general title by a period and a space.

71

> Canada : an encyclopaedia of the country : the Canadian Dominion considered
> in its historic relations, its natural resources, its material progress, and its
> national development. Volume 4

The conventions for a document in several units with individual titles are given in Rule
116.

Supplement

72

A supplement is a document published as an adjunct to another publication. For
example, some school textbooks are supplemented by a teacher handbook and student
workbooks. The supplement is linked to the main document by common authorship,
common title or statement of intent in the supplement. When the title of the main
document is not grammatically related to the title of the supplement, the title of the main
document should be recorded, followed by a period, a space, and the supplement title.

> 1001 traps in French grammar and idioms
> *main document title*

> 1001 traps in French grammar and idioms. Teacher's guide
> *Supplement title*

> The lure of the Labrador wild
> *Main document title*

> Bared boughs and grieving winds : a guide to The lure of the Labrador wild : a
> source book for teachers & students
> *Supplement title*

Document in Tumble or Tête-Bêche Format

73

If a bilingual document is bound in tumble or tête-bêche format and thus contains two
title pages, the main source of information used for creating the entry is normally the
title page that is in the language of the bibliography's intended users. The title from the
other title page is recorded in the notes field, preceded by the expression "Title of
additional t.p." Tumble or tête-bêche format is often used in publications by the
Canadian government and international organizations (see Chapter 6, "Bilingual Documents").

Entry under Title

A bibliographic entry begins with the title field if any of the following three conditions apply:

1) The name of the person responsible for the document's intellectual or artistic content does not appear in the work and cannot be determined from any other source:

   Dreadful wreck of the brig St. Lawrence, from Quebec to New York, 1780, which struck on an island of ice [...]

2) The document is produced by a corporate body but is not of an administrative nature or reflective of the group's collective thought or activity.

   Elements of the drama. – Vancouver : British Columbia Teachers Federation

3) The role of the person named in the main source of information (e.g., an editor or producer) is limited to coordinating the contributions of other individuals.

   Readings in Canadian geography. – Edited by Robert M. Irving

Section 3
Secondary Authors

Definition

75

A "secondary author" is a person or corporate body who played a subsidiary role in the creation of the document.

Punctuation

76

When this field contains two or more personal or corporate names, they are separated by a comma and a space.

The field is closed by a period, space, en dash and another space.

Recording Rules

77

Personal names in the secondary author field are recorded in their regular sequence, and not reversed as in the author field. Also recorded is a brief description of the secondary author's contribution, as indicated in the main source of information. If the nature of this contribution is not specified in the main source of information, it should be enclosed in brackets in the entry.

Main Functions of Secondary Authors

78

A "secondary author" may be:

- an **artist** who collaborated with a writer on a document:

      Wynne-Jones, Tim. – Architect of the moon. – Pictures by Ian Wallace

- the **writer** of a musical work with lyrics:

      Surdin, Morris. – The arithmetic of love [music]. – Lyrics by W.O. Mitchell

- the **illustrator** of a book:

      Ahlberg, Allan. – Each peach pear plum. – [Illustrations] Janet Ahlberg

In the last example, Janet Ahlberg's function as an illustrator does not appear in the chief source of information. To avoid any confusion the word "illustrations" is added in square brackets to indicate that this term does not appear in the chief source of information.

- the **interviewer** in a document with a question-and-answer format:

> Gould, Glenn. – Conversations with Glenn Gould. – Introduction and interviews by Jonathan Cott.

- the **annotator** of a text that is longer than its accompanying commentary:

> Lampman, Archibald. – The story of an affinity. – Edited by D.M.R. Bentley

- a **translator**:

> Lemelin, Roger. – The Plouffe family. – Translated from the French by Mary Finch

- the **author** of a foreword, preface, introduction or afterword:

> Flanagan, Robert. – Incisions. – Preface by Margaret Atwood

- the **editor** of a collection:

> Parliament and Canadian foreign policy. – Edited by David Taras

- the **producer** of a motion picture, video recording or slide presentation:

> My American cousin [motion picture]. – Produced by Peter O'Brian

- a **performer**, (i.e., the **artist** in a sound recording of works by one composer, or the **orchestra** and **conductor** in a sound recording of works by one composer or in an untitled sound recording of works by various composers):

> Handel, George Frideric. – Six concerti grossi, opus 3 [audio recording]. – Boyd Neel Orchestra, Boyd Neel, conductor, Thurston Dart, harpsichord and organ

- the **writer** of a document produced for a corporate body:

> Grand Council of the Crees (of Quebec). – What the land provides : an examination of the Fort George subsistence economy and the possible consequences on it of the James Bay hydroelectric project. – Prepared by Martin S. Weinstein

- a **corporate** body that commissioned a document:

> Penfold, Judith. – Early blowouts. – For the Western Natural Gas Foundation Committee on Archives

Section 4
Edition

Definition

79

An "edition" is all the copies of a document that are produced from the same master copy. When the master copy is changed (except in a minor way, e.g., to correct typographical errors), the new copies produced constitute another edition. Edition information (found in the main source of information) may consist of an edition number, with or without a brief description of the changes in the text from the previous edition, or an edition designation.

> Second edition
>
> 5th edition, revised and enlarged
>
> National edition
>
> 1st Canadian edition

Edition information does not include "impression" (also known as "imprint" and "printing") or "reprint" information. An impression is the set of copies produced in one print run, and a reprint is a work republished by its original publisher in a new format or reproduced by a second publisher who has acquired reprint rights. An edition may thus comprise several impressions (printings) or reprintings (e.g., deluxe edition, numbered edition, paperback edition).

As a general rule, only the edition information is recorded. Occasionally, reprint information is provided in a note. However, only in exceptional cases (e.g., a rare book) are printing details included in the entry.

Punctuation

80

The edition field ends with a period, space, en dash and another space.

Recording Rules

Edition information is recorded in the bibliographic entry as it appears in the main source of information. However, the edition number should be expressed in Arabic numerals, even if it is given in letters in the main source of information. Standard abbreviations are used if they will not create confusion. A list of standard bibliographic abbreviations is given in the Appendix. Additional abbreviations can be found in *Acronyms, initialisms & abbreviations dictionary*, ed. Julie E. Towell.[*]

81

> 2nd ed.
>
> 5th ed., rev. and enl.
>
> School ed.

Works in Other Languages

For a bilingual document, edition information should be recorded in the language of the bibliography's intended users. Thus, if the document provides edition information in both French and English, only the information in English will appear in a bibliography intended for Anglophones (see Chapter 6, "Bilingual Documents").

82

For works in languages other than the language of the bibliography, the edition information is recorded in the language used in the work. Depending on the purpose of the bibliography and the needs of its intended users, a translation of the edition information may be included in the entry.

> Kiriak, Illia. – Syny Zemli [Sons of the soil]. – 2 vyd. [2nd ed.]

(For a discussion of translation and romanization, see Chapter 3, Sections 4 and 5.)

Document Revised or Enlarged by Person Other Than Author

If a document has been revised, edited, corrected or enlarged by a person other than the original author, the name of the reviser is entered in the edition field after the edition information. It is recorded in its regular sequence, not in reverse order. The name of the original author appears in the author field.

83

> Saunders, Chas. E. – The best varieties of grain. – Revised by L.H. Newman

---

[*] *See Bibliography.*

Document in Several Units and Several Editions

84

When the entry refers to a document consisting of several units (e.g., a multivolume work), which are not all in the same edition, information on the different editions should be included in a note.

> English historical documents. – General editor, David C. Douglas. – London: E. Methuen, 1979-1981. – 12 vol. – Vol. 1-2, second edition. – ISBN 0-413-32500-8

Successive Editions

85

When several editions of the same work are listed in a bibliography, each edition is recorded in a separate entry.

> Birney, Earle. – Turvey : a military picaresque. Toronto : McClelland & Stewart, 1949. – 288 p.
>
> Birney, Earle. – Turvey : a military picaresque. – Revised edition. – Toronto : McClelland and Stewart, 1976. – 288 p. – ISBN 0-7710-1412-0.

Section 5
Issue Designation

Definition

The issue designation consists of the volume or issue number and the publication date of a serial publication that are relevant to a bibliography. Note that this information is given only in entries for serial publications (e.g., serial runs of periodicals, newspapers, and such annual publications as reports, yearbooks and conference proceedings). The issue designation field (e.g., an issue of an annual report) is also used in entries for single issues or parts of serial publications (e.g., periodical articles).

86

Punctuation

Number elements are separated by a comma and a space.

The issue date is enclosed in parentheses.

The hyphen (-) may serve one of two functions: to separate consecutive sequences of volume or issue numbers or dates, in which case it is not preceded or followed by a space; or to indicate that publication of the document is ongoing, in which case the hyphen is followed by four spaces.

A slash (/) is used to separate consecutive numbers or dates within a set of issue numbers or dates.

The semicolon (;) separates non-consecutive issue numbers or dates.

The field is closed by a period, space, en dash and another space.

87

Recording Rules

The issue designation is recorded as completely as possible and includes one or more of the following: volume, number, season, part, section, day, week, month, year. Numbers are expressed in Arabic form, even if they appear in Roman numerals in the main source of information, and standard abbreviations are used. A list of standard

88

bibliographic abbreviations is given in the Appendix, and additional abbreviations can be found in Chapter One of *The Canadian style: a guide to writing and editing.*[*]

Several Consecutive Issues

89

In an entry for all the issues of an ongoing serial publication, the issue designation data for the first issue is recorded, followed by a hyphen and four spaces. (In the examples below, spaces are represented by the symbol "▮".)

> Vol. 1, no. 1 (Jan. 1960)-▮▮▮▮. –
>
> (Winter 1972)-▮▮▮▮. –
>
> Vol. 1, no. 1 (Fall/Winter 1980)-▮▮▮▮. –

If the numbering system for a serial publication has been changed at some point during the life of the publication, the issue designation field should list all the numbering systems, separated by a semicolon preceded and followed by a space (;).

> Vol. 1, no. 1 (Jan./Feb. 1977)-vol. 3, no. 5 (Sept./Oct. 1980) ;
> vol. 1, no. 1 (Nov. 1980)-

In an entry for a serial that has ceased publication or for a limited number of consecutive issues, the hyphen is followed by the designation of the last issue published or the last issue in the series cited. In both cases, there is no space before or after the hyphen.

> Serial that has ceased publication:
>
> No. 1 (Jan. 1974)-no. 41 (Jan. 1984)
>
> Limited number of issues:
>
> Vol. 1, no. 1 (Oct. 1978)-vol. 2, no. 2 (Jan. 1980)
>
> Vol. 6, no. 20 (Fall 1974)-vol. 14, no. 63 (Spring 1984)
>
> (1972/1973)-(1985/1986)

One Serial Issue or Part

90

For one issue of a serial publication or part of a single issue, the issue designation field should record as specifically as possible the number and date of the issue or the title of the issue that contains the part. The hyphen is omitted.

> Vol. 8, no. 3 (March 1987)
>
> No. 4 (Winter 1986)

---

[*] *See Bibliography.*

Section 6
Publication Data

Definition

Publication data consists of the place of publication, the name of the publisher and the year of publication.

91

> Toronto : McClelland and Stewart, 1983

Publication data is generally found in the main source of information. However, some information may appear on other parts of the document (e.g., a book cover, record sleeve or motion- picture can). If no publication data appears in the document, refer to Rules 96, 103, 104 and 106.

Punctuation

A colon preceded and followed by a space (:) separates the names of the place and publisher, and the names of copublishers in the same location.

92

The semicolon (;), preceded and followed by a space, is used to separate each set of place and publisher when the item is co-published and the publishers are in different locations.

A comma followed by a space (,) separates the publisher's name from the date of publication.

The hyphen (-) is used immediately after the publication date. Followed by four spaces, it indicates that publication is ongoing. It may also be inserted without spaces between the first and last dates of publication of a document published in several parts over several years.

The field ends with a period, space, en dash and another space.

Place of Publication

Recording Rules

The place of publication is recorded in the entry as it appears in the document.

93

> Montréal OR Montreal

Additions to Place-Names

94

When the place-name is not well known or could be confused with another place-name, the entry should provide additional information, usually the name of the larger geographic jurisdiction in which the city is located.

The additional information may be given in abbreviated form if it will not confuse the bibliography's users. Standard abbreviations of place-names in Canada and the United States are listed under Rule 154. As specified in Rules 10 and 11, the additional information is enclosed in parentheses if taken from the document, and in brackets if taken from another source.

> London (Ont.)
>
> Edmundston [N.B.]

Several Places of Publication

95

If a document lists more than one place of publication (e.g., a publisher with offices in several cities), only the first place-name is recorded in the entry.

No Place of Publication Listed

96

When the place of publication is not listed in the document but is known from another source or can be deduced, it is recorded in brackets in the publication data field.

> Bishop, Charles W. – The Canadian Y.M.C.A. in the Great War : the official record of the activities of the Canadian Y.M.C.A. in connection with the Great War of 1914-1918. – [Toronto]

If there is no way of determining the place of publication, the notation "S.l." ("sine loco", meaning "without place") should appear in the entry. The "S" is capitalized, the "l" is given in lower case, and both are enclosed in brackets.

> Young Women's Christian Association of Canada. – Basic information manual. – [S.l.]

Publisher

Recording Rules

97

The publisher's name is recorded in the entry as it appears in the document. The entry should faithfully reproduce capitalization and internal punctuation.

> Thunder Enlightening Press
>
> blewointmentpress
>
> Macmillan NOT MacMillan
>
> Clarke, Irwin NOT Clarke Irwin or Clarke and Irwin

McClelland & Stewart   OR   McClelland and Stewart

If the publisher's name has been changed since the date of publication, the entry should nevertheless record the name found in the work.

Abbreviations

Publishers' names are usually abbreviated in the following ways:

98

1) An article as the first word in the name (e.g., "The") is omitted.

> Canadian Bar Association

and not

> The Canadian Bar Association

2) Terms such as "Ltd.", "Co." and "Inc." are also omitted.

> General Publishing

and not

> The General Publishing Co.

3) When the publisher is the author of the work, the name is abbreviated in the publication data field (see below).

Author as Publisher

When the work has been published by its personal author, the author's initial and surname are recorded as the publisher's name.

99

> McNichol, Vera Ernst. – Reveries of a pioneer : Blanshard and Downie. – Millbank (Ont.) : V. McNichol

Similarly, if a document has been published by its corporate author, the corporate name is recorded in abbreviated form.

> National Capital Commission. – A very special mandate : shaping Canada's capital : the story of the National   Capital Commission. – [Ottawa] : the Commission

Publisher with Subordinate Levels

If the work is issued by a subordinate corporate body, the name of the parent body is also listed as the publisher. The names of the different levels are recorded in the same order as given in the document and are separated by a comma.

100

> Hosie, R.C. – Native Trees of Canada. – Ottawa : Canadian Forestry Service, Department of the Environment

Publisher's Name in Several Languages

101

If the publisher's name appears in more than one language in the document, it should be recorded in the language of the document title. However, for a bilingual document, the publisher's name is recorded in the language of the bibliography's intended users. Thus, when a publisher's name appears in English and French, a bibliography intended for Anglophone users records the English versions of the name (see Chapter 6, "Bilingual Documents").

Co-publishers

102

For a document with two or more publishers, the names are entered in the same order as they appear in the document. However, if one of the names is more prominently presented in the document, it should be listed before the others in the entry. Units consisting of place-name and publisher name are separated by a semicolon.

> Toronto : McClelland and Stewart ; New York : Knopf
>
> The names of publishers in the same location are separated by a colon.
>
> Ottawa : Footprints of Heritage : Wellspring Press

No Publisher Listed

103

When the publisher's name is not indicated in the document, the entry should contain the notation "s.n." ("sine nomine", meaning "without name"). Both letters are given in lower case and enclosed in brackets.

> The blue book or Statement of the public service of the former Province of Canada, for the half-year ended 30th June, 1867. – Ottawa : [s.n.]

No Place of Publication or Publisher Name Listed

104

When neither the place of publication nor the publisher's name appear in the document, all the information provided by the bibliographer in the entry is enclosed in a single set of brackets.

> Beecroft, Jane. – Paradox. – Etchings by Jo Manning. – [S.l. : s.n.], 1974

Publication Date

Recording Rules

105

The only date recorded in the entry is usually the year of publication, not the month or day. These elements may, however, be included in entries for documents containing information that is rapidly outdated in some technical fields. The date is expressed in Arabic numerals, even if it is given in Roman numerals in the document.

No Publication Date Listed

When no publication date appears in the work, the entry should contain one of the elements listed below in order of preference.

1) The copyright date, preceded by the letter "c" or the symbol ©. There is no space between the letter or symbol and the date:

   Montgomery, L.M. – Anne of Ingleside. – Toronto : McClelland & Stewart, c1939

2) The impression or printing date

3) An estimated publication date, followed by a question mark and enclosed in brackets:

   Wolfe, J.S., et al. – Farm family financial crisis : overview of impacts and responses. – Guelph, Ont. : University of Guelph, University School of Rural Planning and Development, [1988?]

4) The notation "s.d." (sine die, meaning "without date"):

   Scott, Anna Lee. – Cooking made easy. – Toronto : Maple Leaf Milling, [s.d.]

Document in Several Units

1) Published over several years — For a work comprising two or more units published over a period of years, the entry records the first and last publication dates, separated by an en dash. Examples of documents in this category are a multivolume work, a serial that has ceased publication, and a limited number of periodical issues.

   Creative Canada : a biographical dictionary of twentieth-century creative and performing artists. – Compiled by Reference Division, McPherson Library, University of Victoria. – Toronto : University of Toronto Press, 1971-1972

   Quest. – Vol. 1, no. 1 (May 1972)-vol. 13, no. 8 (Dec. 1984). – Toronto : Comac Communications, 1972-1984

2) Still being published — If one or more units of the document have been published, but others have yet to be published, the date of the first unit is entered, followed by a hyphen and four spaces. In the examples below, spaces are represented by the symbol "∎".

   The annotated bibliography of Canada's major authors. Edited by Robert Lecker and Jack David. – Downsview, Ont. : ECW Press, 1979-∎∎∎∎

3) Published in the same year — If all the units of the document were published in the same year and are recorded as one entry in the bibliography, the publication date, copyright date or printing date, in that order of preference, should be cited.

   The Canadian Encyclopedia. – 2nd ed. – Edmonton : Hurtig, 1988

No Publication Data Listed

If a document does not list the place of publication, the publisher or the publication date, the notations for these missing elements are recorded in brackets in the entry.

Purdy, Al. – Nine bean-rows on the moon. – [S.l. : s.n., s.d.]

Section 7
Extent

Definition

The extent is the length of the work or the number of units contained in the document. The extent field may include information related to the type of equipment required to consult the document (e.g., the size of a motion-picture film — 8 mm or 16 mm).

> 109

    The information to be recorded in the extent field for each document type is given in Part Two of the manual.

Punctuation

A comma separates the elements of information.

> 110

The field ends with a period, space, en dash and another space.

Recording Rules

Number of Units in Document

The entry records the number of document units and a descriptor. The number is always expressed in Arabic numerals, and the descriptor is given in lower case. Abbreviations are used for pages and volumes.

> 111

       1 sound recording

       3 microfiches

       16 vol.

       327 p.

       72 slides

Number of Units in Document Still Being Published

For a document that is still being published, the number of document units is replaced by three spaces, followed by the descriptor. In the examples below, spaces are represented by the symbol "▮".

▮▮▮vol.
▮▮▮microforms

Section 8
Series

Definition

A series is a number of separate works connected by one or more common factors (e.g., author, subject, theme) and published in succession under a collective or general title. The series title and the number of the work within the series may appear in the main source of information or elsewhere on the document (e.g., the book cover or record sleeve).

113

Punctuation

Series information is enclosed in parentheses.
    A semicolon preceded and followed by a space (;) appears before the numbering.
    A period followed by a space (.) separates series from subseries information.
    The field ends with a period, space, en dash and another space.

114

Recording Rules

The series field records the title of the series and, if applicable, the number of the document within the series. When a document number is accompanied by a term such as "volume" or "number", a standard abbreviation is used (i.e., "vol." or "no."). The abbreviated term, preceded by a space, semicolon and another space, follows the last word of the series title. The number is expressed in Arabic numerals, even if it appears in Roman numerals in the document.

115

    Rasky, Frank. – Great Canadian Disasters. – Don Mills, Ont. : Longman
    Canada, 1970. – 246 p. – (Windjammer Books ; no. 7)

Document in Several Units with Individual Titles

116

For an individually titled work that is part of a series, the individual title should be entered in the title field. The series title and the number of the work within the series are recorded in the series field.

> United Canada, 1840-1867. – Adam Shortt, Arthur G. Doughty, general editors. – Toronto : Glasglow, Brook, 1914. – 404 p. – (Canada and its provinces ; vol. 5)

For a document in several units with no individual titles, see Rule 71 ("Document in Several Units under General Title Only").

Several Numbers

117

When all the works of a series are cited in one entry, the numbers of the first and last are listed if the numbering is consecutive, and the numbers of all the works are listed if the numbering is discontinuous.

> Burt, A.L. – The old province of Quebec. – Introd. Hilda Neatby. – Toronto : McClelland and Stewart, 1968. – 2 vols. – (Carleton Library ; 37-38)

Subseries

118

A series may contain one or more subseries, described by a numbering system, a word, a phrase or a combination of numbers and words. All this information should appear in the entry. The subseries title is separated from the series by a period and a space.

> McCallum, Heather. – Theatre – resources in Canadian collections. – Ottawa : National Library of Canada, 1973. 113 p. – (Research Collections in Canadian Libraries ; II. Special studies ; 1)

Work Belonging to More than One Series

119

When a work is part of two series, both series are listed in the series field, each within parentheses.

> Simpson, George, Sir. – Journal of occurrences in the Athabasca Department by George Simpson, 1820 and 1821, and Report. – Edited by E.E. Rich, foreword by Lord Tweedsmuir, introduction by Chester Martin. – Toronto : The Champlain Society, 1938. – 570 p. in various paginations. (Publications of the Champlain Society) (Hudson's Bay Company Series ; 1)

Section 9
Notes

Definition

The note is a brief item of information, usually taken from the document, supplying relevant details that do not appear elsewhere in the bibliographic entry.

120

Punctuation

Each note ends with a period, space, en dash and another space.

121

Recording Rules

Not every bibliographic entry should include notes. They are used only to provide essential or useful information, and should be as brief and concise as possible. Whether a note is deemed necessary and what elements it should contain will depend on the nature and purpose of the bibliography, and the needs of its intended users.

122

Purposes of Notes

Notes are used mainly to:

1) indicate the original title of a work that has been translated or adapted.

123

> Grandbois, Alain. – Born in Quebec : a tale of Louis Jolliet. – Translated from the French by Evelyn M. Brown. – Montreal : Palm Publishers, c1964. – 198 p. – Translation of Né à Québec : Louis Jolliet : récit

2) list the individual works of a document if they are not cited elsewhere in the entry.

> Davies, Robertson. – Eros at breakfast and other plays. – Toronto : Clarke, Irwin, 1949. – Contents: Eros at breakfast, The voice of the people, Hope deferred, Overlaid, At the gates of the righteous

3) record the title appearing on the title page that was not used as the main source of information for a tumble-format document. This title is preceded by the expression "Title of additional t.p.".

> Dallaire, Pierre. – Glossary of baseball terms : English-French, French-English. – Toronto : CBC Enterprises, c1984. 110, 110 p. – Text in English and French with French text on inverted pages. Title of additional t.p.: Répertoire de termes de baseball

4) provide more specific edition information, as in the case of a document with multiple parts where not all the parts are from the same edition.

> English historical documents. – General editor, David C. Douglas. – London: E. Methuen, 1979-1981. – 12 vol. – Vol. 1-2, second edition. – ISBN 0-413-32500-8

5) give information about the original work if the document cited is a reprint.

> Ross, Alexander. – The Red River settlement : its rise, progress, and present state : with some account of the native races and its general history to the present day. – Edmonton : Hurtig, 1972. – 416 p. – Facsimile of 1856 edition

6) identify and describe the work.

> Rivard, Ken. – Kiss me down to size. – Saskatoon : Thistledown Press, c1983. – 77 p. – Poems

> Van de Vyvere, James Lawrence. – Archetypes of the collective unconscious in three novels by John Steinbeck [microform] – Ottawa : National Library of Canada, 1974. – 2 microfiches. – M.A. dissertation, Lakehead University

7) specify the location or source of the document.

> Morgan, Henry J. – Bibliotheca canadensis or A manual of Canadian literature. – Ottawa : G.E. Desbarats, 1867. – Held in Rare Book Room, National Library of Canada, Ottawa

8) provide numbers relevant to the identification of the work (e.g., a stock number or international patent number).

> Baker, Michael C. – The grey fox [sound recording] : original soundtrack. – DRG Records, c1983. – 1 disc, 33 1/3 rpm. – Ed. no.: Concorde Series SL9515

9) indicate the scale of a map.

> Canada. Department of Energy, Mines and Resources. Surveys and Mapping Branch. – Ottawa : Ontario, Quebec. – 10th ed. – Ottawa : the Branch, c1987. – 1 map. – Scale, 1:50 000

10) indicate the presence and type of accompanying materials (e.g., the cassette for a slide presentation).

> Copyright the 80's [sound recording]. – [S.l.]: Continuing Legal Education Society of British Columbia, [s.d.]. – 4 cassettes. – Recording of a seminar held on Feb. 15, 1985. – Includes seminar outline

Section 10
Standard Number

Definition

There are two types of standard international numbers: the International Standard Book Number (ISBN) and the International Standard Serial Number (ISSN).

124

ISBN

The ISBN is a ten-digit number used to identify books, pamphlets, educational kits, multimedia kits, microforms and Braille works. An ISBN consists of four parts.

> ISBN 0-8772-2551-6

Each edition of a work is assigned a unique ISBN because a new edition is, in effect, a work different from the previous edition. The paperback format of a work also has an ISBN that is different from that of the hardcover format, even when the contents are exactly the same; the two ISBNs are intended to distinguish between the two formats when copies of the work are being ordered, bought or sold. The ISBN is thus essential to document identification. If a work lists more than one ISBN, only the ISBN of the work on hand is recorded in the bibliographic entry.

The ISBN may appear on the verso of the title page or on the book cover or jacket. However, it is found only on works published since 1967, when the ISBN system was established.

ISSN

The ISSN is an eight-digit number used to identify serial publications. It consists of two parts.

> ISSN 0831-0300

The ISSN is usually found on the cover or copyright page of each serial issue or with the serial ordering information.

Note that, as the ISSN system was established in 1972, issues before that year do not bear an ISSN.

Both the ISBN and ISSN assist the book trade and libraries in such activities as stock control, ordering and accounting. They are recorded in bibliographic entries because they are also used for location and retrieval in computerized systems.

Punctuation

125

The standard number field does not contain any technical punctuation. Moreover, when it is the last field in the entry, it does not end with technical punctuation (see Rule 7 - "Punctuation between Fields"). However, if the field contains more than one standard number, a comma separates the numbers.

Recording Rules

126

The standard number is recorded after the notes, if any, and is preceded by the letters "ISBN" or "ISSN", in upper case. The parts of the number should be separated by hyphens.

> Curtis, Bo. – Canada from the air. – [Photographs] J.A. Kraulis. – Edmonton : Hurtig, 1981. – 128 p. – ISBN 0888302010

More Than One Standard Number

127

A document may list more than one standard number (e.g., two ISBNs or an ISBN and ISSN).

Two or More ISBNs

If copublishers have each assigned an ISBN to the same document, all the ISBNs appearing in the document should be recorded in the entry, each followed by the name of the respective publisher.

> Virgilio, Nicholas A. – Selected haiku. – 2nd ed., augmented. – Sherbrooke : Burnt Lake Press ; Windsor, Ont. : Black Moss Press, 1988. – 78 p. – ISBN 0-920349-05-6 (Burnt Lake Press), ISBN 0-88753-180-6 (Black Moss Press)

For a document in several units bearing different ISBNs, the entry records the general ISBN for the entire publication if such an ISBN exists; otherwise, all the ISBNs are recorded. When only one unit of the publication is cited, only the ISBN of that unit is recorded.

An ISBN and an ISSN

For a document containing both an ISBN and an ISSN (e.g., if a book bearing an ISBN is published as part of a series that bears an ISSN), the entry should record only the ISBN and not the series ISSN.

However, for a document that is considered to be a serial publication rather than a book (e.g., an annual report), the entry should cite the ISSN, which is often the reference used in computerized systems.

Section 11
Location in Host Document

Definition

128 Used only in an entry for part of a work (e.g., a chapter of a book or an article in a periodical), the location in the host document specifies where the part appears in the work.

Punctuation

129 This field contains no technical punctuation and, as the last field in the entry, does not end with technical punctuation (see Rule 7 — "Punctuation between Fields").

Recording Rules

130 The location in the host document briefly designates the document type and indicates, with a number or numbers, which part of the larger work is being cited. The document type designation is capitalized at the beginning of the field, and abbreviations are used for "pages" and "volumes". Consecutive numbers are separated by an en dash with no spaces, and discontinuous numbers are separated by a comma and a space.

> Microfiche no. 27
>
> P. 32-83
>
> Vol. 16, p. 12-77
>
> Slide no. 22
>
> P. 27, 38-41
>
> P. 22-25, 82

CHAPTER 3

Capitalization, Spelling, Abbreviation, Translation, and Romanization

Section 1
Capitalization

Author

Personal Names

Personal names usually appear in the author field and secondary author field of a bibliographic entry. As a general rule, they are capitalized as in the main source of information. When the work shows no distinct form of capitalization (e.g., when the author's name is given entirely in block capitals), traditional rules of capitalization are applied: the first letter of each forename and surname is capitalized, as are all initials.

131

> Bellware, Jo-Ann
> Chrystos
> Koros, Marcus B.
> Moffat, Julie Elizabeth
> Robert, J.R.
> Tanner, S. Frank

Prefixed Names

If the capitalization of a prefixed name is not clearly presented in the main source of information, it should be determined from other parts of the document (e.g., the book cover or record sleeve) or outside information sources (e.g., standard reference works or publishers' catalogues). It is particularly important for prefixed names to be recorded accurately in entries because capitalization of prefixes varies widely, as indicated by this list of examples.

132

> de Grandpré, Pierre
> de La Corne, Luc
> DesRochers, Alfred
> LaRocque, Gilbert
> Mac Bean, Elizabeth
> MacDonald, Wilson

Macdonald, Malcolm

van der Mark, Christine

Van Kirk, Sylvia

VanOene, W.W.J.

Corporate Names

133

When the author is a corporate body (i.e., a company, association or organization), all nouns, pronouns and adjectives of the name in the entry are capitalized; conjunctions, prepositions and articles are not. However, if a name is consistently presented with a different style of capitalization in the document, that style is given in the entry.

Association of Universities and Colleges of Canada

Bank of Nova Scotia

CBC Vancouver Orchestra

Canadian Imperial Bank of Commerce

Grand Council of the Crees (of Quebec)

National Film Board of Canada

Quebec Bureau of Statistics

Royal Society of Canada

Saskatchewan-Nelson Basin Board

Vincent d'Indy School of Music

Corporate Body Created or Managed by Public Authority

134

The names of corporate bodies (e.g., government departments) created or managed by a public authority follow the same capitalization conventions as do other corporate names: all words in the name are capitalized except for conjunctions, prepositions and articles.

Canada. Public Service Commission

Canada. Department of Finance

Canada. Industry and Commerce

Canada. Department of Industry and Commerce

New Brunswick. Department of Youth and Recreation

New Brunswick. Human Rights Commission

Quebec (Province). Department of Lands, Mines and Fisheries

Quebec (Province). Directorate of School Buildings and Equipment

Title

Document Titles

The first word of titles and alternative titles, and all proper nouns and adjectives are capitalized (except for cases outlined in Rule 138). Other words in the title field should appear in lower case.

135

Titles

A treatise on probability

Great Canadian disasters

Stories about 125 years at Touche, Ross

We stand on guard

Alternative titles

Great housewives of art or Mrs. Gaugin has a Tupperware party

Hochelaga or England in the New World

Wacousta or The prophecy

Western wanderings or Pleasure tour in the Canadas

Subtitles

Machine translation : past, present, future

The organization of the early Christian churches : eight lectures

The settler : a tale of Saskatchewan

Sounds Canadian : languages and cultures in multi-ethnic society

Capitalized Titles

In the titles of some older works, entire words may appear on capitals. However, the capitalization in the entry should be the same as for other document titles (see Rule 135). Thus, the title

136

AN ACCOUNT OF THE LIFE, TRAVELS, AND CHRISTIAN EXPERIENCES IN THE work of the ministry OF SAMUEL BOWNAS is altered to appear in the entry as:

> An account of the life, travels, and Christian experiences in the work of the ministry of Samuel Bownas

Some or all of the words in certain titles may be capitalized. This is ignored in the transcription and the title is entered according to the rules devined above. For instance, the title

> THE CANADIAN ATLAS OF RECREATION AND EXERCISE = L'ATLAS CANADIEN DE LA RECREATION ET DE L'ACTIVITE PHYSIQUE

would be entered as follows:

> The Canadian atlas of recreation and exercise = L'atlas canadien de la récréation et de l'activité physique.

Parallel Titles

137

Capitalization of the parallel title (the title of the work in another language or script) follows the bibliographic conventions of that language.

> Médecine et religion populaires = Folk medicine and religion

> Langage du droit et traduction : essais de jurilinguistique = The language of the law and translation : essays on jurilinguistics

Consistently Unconventional Capitalization

138

If a work consistently presents one or more of the title words with an unusual style of capitalization, that style is given in the entry.

> enRoute

> artmagazine

> NeWest plays by women

Newspaper or Periodical Title

139

The capitalization of newspaper and periodical titles in English-language bibliographic entries is the same as for other document titles (see Rule 135).

Secondary Author

140

In the secondary author field, the capitalization of personal and corporate names follows the conventions of the language in question (see Rules 131 to 134). Other words, except the first word of the field, and any proper nouns and adjectives, are given in lower case.

> Kain & Augustyn. – Photographs by Christopher Darling, text by John Fraser, foreword by Rudolf Nureyev

Edition

A word or abbreviation appearing as the first element in the edition field should be capitalized. Other words may be capitalized, depending on the conventions of the language in question.

141

> Aster, Howard. – Jewish-Ukrainian relations : two solitudes. – Rev. 2nd ed.
>
> Fischer, William L. – How to fight cancer & win. – Rev. Canadian ed.
>
> Grant, John Webster. – The church in the Canadian era. – Updated & expanded.

Issue Designation

The first word or abbreviation in the issue designation field is capitalized, as are all proper nouns and names of seasons. All other words and abbreviations are in lower case.

142

> Vol. 6, no. 6 (Nov./Dec. 1983)-
>
> (Winter 1983)-
>
> No. 15-
>
> Vol. 7, no. 2 (Spring 1982)-
>
> Vol. 6, no. 5 (Nov./Dec. 1983)-vol. 7, no. 5 (Sept./Oct. 1985)
>
> (Summer 1983)-(Winter 1984)

Publication Data

Place-Names

Whether spelled out or abbreviated, all place-names are capitalized.

143

> Winnipeg
> Edmundston (N.B.)
> Camrose [Alberta]

Publisher's Name

Personal or corporate names in the publication data field are capitalized according to the conventions of the language in question (see Rules 131 to 134). The abbreviated name of a corporate author-publisher (e.g., "Department" or "Committee" — see Rule 155) is also capitalized.

144

> Metric Commission Canada. – How to write SI = Petit manuel des unités SI. – 6th ed. – Ottawa : the Commission, 1982

Series

145 The titles of series are capitalized in the same way as are document titles (see Rule 135): The first word of the title is capitalized, as are all proper nouns and adjectives. All other words are given in lower case. Series rarely have alternative titles.

Makers of Canada Series

McGill Social Research Series

Essay Index Reprint Series

Frontenac Library

Carleton Library

Civilization of the American Indian

Notes

146 Capitalization in a note follows the conventions of the language: The first word and all proper nouns and adjectives are capitalized.

French title: Les tâches liées au soin des enfants

Poems in English and Hungarian on facing pages

Originally published in London by the Institute of

Economic Affairs with the title From Galbraith to economic freedom

Standard Number

147 The initialisms for international standard numbers are given in block capitals.

ISBN 2-89198-044-1

ISSN 0226-7572

Location in Host Document

148 Only the designation of the document type at the beginning of the field is capitalized.

P. 221-337

Vol. 3, p. 12-75

Microfiche no. 3

Slide no. 25

Section 2
Spelling

The bibliographic entry should retain the spelling that appears in the work. Fidelity to the work is particularly important with regard to personal names (of authors and secondary authors), corporate names (of authors, publishers and sponsoring agencies) and document titles.

149

Names of persons

Thibault, Diane

Thibeault, Jacques

Tibo

Dropaôt, Papartchu

Names of corporate bodies

Bizy Graphikos

blewointmentpress

Cranberrie Publications

Writers' Union of Canada

Canadian Authors Association

Titles

The man with 7 toes

up her can nada

If there are several versions of a name in a bibliography, as sometimes occurs when a name has been romanized in various works, one version should be chosen and recorded consistently throughout the bibliography. When several elements in a bibliographic entry are romanized, the same romanization system should be used for all the elements (see Section 5 of this chapter.)

Older Works

If the title of an older work contains words whose spelling or typography differs from the form in use today, they may be altered in the entry to reflect current usage. For instance, the title

> The History of travayle in the VVest and East Indies, and other countreys lying eyther way, towards the fruitfull and rich Molluccaes [...]

could be changed to:

> The history of travail in the West and East Indies, and other countries lying either way, towards the fruitful and rich Moluccas [...]

Any such changes, however, should be indicated in a note:

> The spelling of some words in the title has been changed.

Section 3
Abbreviations

General Conventions

Abbreviations of bibliographic terms may be used in an entry when their meanings are clearly defined and presented. Ambiguous and potentially confusing abbreviations should be avoided.

150

When abbreviations are used, the bibliography should supply a key to their meanings if they can refer to more than one term. For example, "ed." could signify "edition" or "editor". When an abbreviation has been used with a certain meaning, it should retain that meaning throughout the bibliography.

This section provides guidelines for abbreviating document titles, numbers, and the names of months, places and publishers. A list of standard bibliographic terms and their recommended abbreviations is given in the Appendix.

Additional information on the abbreviation of bibliographic terms and of terms that are not directly related to bibliography can be found in various reference works, including T. Dobroslavic and S. Yates, *Abbreviations: a Canadian handbook*; Ralph De Sola, ed., *Abbreviations dictionary* (Expanded international 6th ed.), *Documentation, bibliographical references, abbreviations of typical words* (ISO 832-1975), published by the International Organization for Standardization.[*]

All abbreviations are followed by a period unless otherwise indicated.

Document Titles

As stated in Rule 66 ("Abridgement of Title"), abridged, or abbreviated, titles are used sparingly because they are potentially confusing. Titles should be abbreviated only if the space for the bibliography is limited.

151

Abbreviated titles should always retain the first few words of the original title, and the omitted words are replaced by an ellipsis in brackets. Standard abbreviated titles for periodicals can be found in reference sources such as *American National Standard for*

---

[*] *See Bibliography.*

the abbreviation of titles of periodicals (ANSI Z39.5-1985) (issued by the American National Standards Institute) for documents in English and *Documentation — règles pour l'abréviation des mots dans les titres et des titres des publications* (ISO 4-1984 (F)) for documents in French.[*]

Numbers

152

Ordinal adjectives are abbreviated by adding the letters "th" to the corresponding Arabic numerals, except for the numbers 1, 2 and 3, and numbers ending in 1, 2 or 3 (e.g., 21st).

First	1st
Second	2nd
Third	3rd
Fourth	4th
Seventh	7th

Names of Months

153

The names of months usually appear in the issue designation field. Those that are abbreviated are listed below in English and French.

English		**French**	
January	Jan.	janvier	janv.
February	Feb.	février	févr.
March	Mar.	juillet	juil.
April	Apr.	septembre	sept.
August	Aug.	octobre	oct.
September	Sept.	novembre	nov.
October	Oct.	décembre	déc.
November	Nov.		
December	Dec.		

---

[*] *See Bibliography.*

Place-Names

The names of Canadian provinces and territories are recorded in the language in which they appear in the work. Abbreviations of these names (see below) are used, generally in the publication data field, to provide additional information when a place-name is not well known or could be confused with another place-name.

154

English

Alberta	Alta.
British Columbia	B.C.
Manitoba	Man.
New Brunswick	N.B.
Newfoundland	Nfld.
Northwest Territories	N.W.T.
Nova Scotia	N.S.
Ontario	Ont.
Prince Edward Island	P.E.I.
Saskatchewan	Sask.
Yukon Territory	Yukon

French

Alberta	Alb.
Colombie-Britannique	C.-B.
Île-du-Prince-Édouard	Î.-P.-É.
Manitoba	Man.
Nouveau-Brunswick	N.-B.
Nouvelle-Écosse	N.-É.
Ontario	Ont.
Saskatchewan	Sask.
Terre-Neuve	T.-N.
Territoires du Nord-Ouest	T.N.-O.

The abbreviated names of the American states may also appear in the publication data field. Note that the two-letter postal abbreviation is not used in bibliographies. Rather, the names of American states are abbreviated as follows:

Alabama	Ala.	Montana	Mont.
Alaska	Alas.	Nebraska	Neb.
Arizona	Ariz.	Nevada	Nev.
Arkansas	Ark.	New Hampshire	N.H.
California	Calif.	New Jersey	N.J.

Colorado	Colo.	New Mexico	N.M.
Connecticut	Conn.	New York	N.Y.
Delaware	Del.	North Carolina	N.C.
District of Columbia	D.C.	North Dakota	N.D.
Florida	Fla.	Ohio	O.
Georgia	Ga.	Oklahoma	Okla.
Hawaii	Ha.	Oregon	Or.
Idaho	Ida.	Pennsylvania	Pa.
Illinois	Ill.	Rhode Island	R.I.
Indiana	Ind.	South Carolina	S.C.
Iowa	Ia.	South Dakota	S.D.
Kansas	Kan.	Tennessee	Tenn.
Kentucky	Ky.	Texas	Tex.
Louisiana	La.	Utah	Ut.
Maine	Me.	Vermont	Vt.
Maryland	Md.	Virginia	Va.
Massachusetts	Mass.	Washington	Wash.
Michigan	Mich.	West Virginia	W.Va.
Minnesota	Minn.	Wisconsin	Wis.
Mississippi	Miss.	Wyoming	Wyo.
Missouri	Mo.		

Publisher names

As stated in Rule 98, the only elements omitted from the publisher's name are the preliminary article and terms such as "Ltd.", "Co." and "Inc.".

> Clarke, Irwin & Company Limited

becomes

> Clark, Irwin

> The Cherry Tree Press

appears in the entry as

> Cherry Tree Press

The publisher's name may be abbreviated if the publisher is also the author of the document. When the author-publisher is a person, the publication data field lists the initial and surname. For a corporate author-publisher, the field records the generic designation of the corporate body.

> Barkman, Jean. – Lake Okanagan reflections. – Kelowna, B.C. : J. Barkman, 1987

> Canadian Education Association. – Student transportation in Canada : facts and figures. – Toronto : the Association, 1987

Section 4
Translation

General Conventions

Some bibliographic elements are translated to make the entry more intelligible to users. Like a note, translation supplements the information given in other elements of the entry. It is valuable when the work is in a language that may be unfamiliar to the bibliography's users. Therefore, the decision to provide a translation should be based primarily on a careful consideration of the bibliography's intended audience and their linguistic knowledge.

156

When a translation of some elements is supplied, it should be presented clearly and logically, both within the entry and throughout the bibliography. Thus, if a certain part is translated in one entry, it should also be translated wherever it appears in the other entries.

In entries for foreign-language documents, capitalization and punctuation are governed by the conventions of that language. The bibliographer should, therefore, know and use these conventions, particularly for recording the names of persons, corporate bodies and places, and the titles of documents, editions and series. For example, although most European languages capitalize only the first word and all proper nouns in a document title, exceptions and variations appear from language to language: Common nouns are capitalized in German, as are proper adjectives in Dutch and some personal pronouns in Danish. Consequently, it is essential for the bibliographer to be aware of the rules or traditions peculiar to the language of the work cited.

Elements to be Translated

Title

The title is the bibliographic element most crucial to the identification of the work. If translated, it should accurately reflect the original title and provide sufficient information for the needs of the bibliography's users. Moreover, a supplied translation should be consistent with any translation or citation that may appear in the text itself.

157

The translated title is given in brackets after the original title. There is a space before the opening bracket and another space after the closing bracket. Capitalization of the translated title follows the conventions of the language of the translation (see Rule 135). If a translation is given for the title of part of a document, it is not enclosed in quotation marks.

Shul.han 'Arukh [The set table]

Other Elements

158

In addition to the title of the work, any other element may be translated if warranted by the purpose and scope of the bibliography and the needs of its intended users. Translations of other elements are presented in the same way as title translations, within brackets after the original information, and capitalized and abbreviated according to the conventions in Sections 1 and 3 of this chapter.

2., Aufl. [2nd ed.]

Notes

159

Since notes are intended to assist the bibliography's users, they are given in the language of the bibliography and are subject to the conventions for capitalization detailed in Rules 146 and 150-155.

Section 5
Romanization

General Conventions

The decision to romanize (i.e., to substitute Latin characters for characters that belong to a non-Latin alphabet) depends primarily on the equipment used to produce the final version of the bibliography. If the equipment (e.g., the word processor or printing press) cannot reproduce the non-Latin script in question, the non-Latin material will have to be romanized.

160

The equipment should be able to reproduce any accents or diacritical marks required as part of the romanized version. Otherwise, the necessary marks will have to be inserted by hand in the final or master copy of the bibliography. For example, romanization of certain languages may require one or more of the following characters:

Æ æ Ŀ ŀ Ñ ñ Ś ś Ū ū

Romanization Systems

The ultimate purpose of romanization in a bibliographic entry is to make the entry intelligible to the user of the bibliography. To this end, a system for romanizing should be selected, used consistently throughout the bibliography and cited in a note at the head of the bibliography.

161

Romanization systems for most languages using non-Latin alphabets are given in issues of the *Cataloging service bulletin*, published by Processing Services of the Library of Congress. The nature and intended audience of the bibliography may require additions or modifications to the LC system. Any such changes should be described in a note at the head of the bibliography. The following publications of the International Organization for Standardization may also provide assistance in romanizing elements:

> *Documentation — transliteration of Slavic Cyrillic characters into Latin characters* (ISO 9)

> *Documentation — transliteration of Arabic characters into Latin characters* (ISO 233)

Documentation — transliteration of Hebrew characters into Latin characters (ISO 259)

Documentation — romanization of Chinese (ISO 7098)[*]

"Popular" and "Systematic" Romanization

Discrepancies between "popular" romanization and "systematic", or literal, romanization should be taken into account, particularly in author names or document titles. For example, should each letter of an author's name be given in its standard Latin equivalent as specified in romanization tables, or should the name appear in the form that is preferred by the author or by which the author is known?

Consider the following:

Have Rozenfarb is the systematic romanization according to the Library of Congress system.

Chawa Rosenfarb is the romanized version of the author's name that appears in one of her works.

Chaveh Rosenfarb is the version used in a standard reference work.

After one form of the author's name is chosen, it should be used consistently throughout the bibliography, and cross-references should be provided.

Rosenfarb, Chaveh   **SEE**   Rozenfarb, Have
Rosenfarb, Chawa   **SEE**   Rozenfarb, Have

Capitalization in Foreign Languages

Capitalization and punctuation of romanized texts follow the conventions of the language of the document. For instance, capitalization guidelines for Cyrillic are generally similar to the capitalization rules for French. Other non-Latin languages, such as Arabic, Chinese and Japanese, do not employ capital letter forms, and certain capitalization conventions thus need to be established when information from works in these languages is romanized and recorded. Like the romanization system, the capitalization and punctuation systems used should be described in a note at the head of the bibliography.

---

[*] *See Bibliography.*

Translation in Romanized Entries

Depending on the purpose of the bibliography and the needs of the intended users, the romanized elements in an entry may be translated. As discussed in the section entitled "Translation", the title is the bibliographic element most crucial to the identification of a work. Other elements that are essential to identification should also be translated.

164

PART TWO

CHAPTER 4
Document Formats

Section 1
Books, Book Parts and Pamphlets

A bibliographic entry for a book or pamphlet contains the fields and elements shown in Illustration no. 8. The field numbers are those described in the general entry outline in Rule 3.

1. Scope

This section establishes the conventions for entries for books and pamphlets (i.e., printed documents containing fewer than 49 pages). Part 5 of this section explains how to create an entry for a book part.

2. Bibliographic Information Source

The information required to create an entry for a book or pamphlet usually appears on the title page or title page verso. Some information (e.g., the series title) may also appear on the cover or dust jacket of the work. If these sources do not list all the bibliographic information, it may be taken from reference works or publishers' catalogues, in which case it should be enclosed in brackets, in accordance with Rule 11.

3. Special Bibliographic Features

The bibliographic elements required in entries for books or pamphlets are given in Part One of this manual, with the exception of the extent field, which is described below.

The extent field in an entry for a book or pamphlet lists the length of the work. It consists of a number (or numbers) and an abbreviation for "pages" (if the document is printed on both sides of each sheet), "sheets" (if the document is printed on one side only), "columns" (if the work is printed in numbered columns), or "volumes" (if the work comprises several physical units). The abbreviation is in lower case, unless it appears at the beginning of the field.

No.	FIELD	ELEMENTS
1.	Author Personal or corporate name. –	Dewdney, Selwyn. –
2.	Title Title alternative title : subtitle = parallel title. –	Wind without rain. –
3.	Secondary authors Name of translator, illustrator, editor. –	Introd. John Stevens. –
4.	Edition Number descriptor	
6.	Publication data Place : publisher, date. –	Toronto : McClelland and Stewart, c1974. –
7.	Extent Number of pages or volumes. –	506 p. –
8.	Series (Title ; numbering). –	(New Canadian Library ; 103). –
9.	Notes Additional information. –	
10.	Standard number	ISBN 0-7710-9203-2

Dewdney, Selwyn. – Wind without rain. – Introd. John Stevens. Toronto : McClelland and Stewart, c1974. – 506 p. – (New Canadian Library ; 103). – ISBN 0-7710-9203-2

Illustration no. 9 lists various forms of books and pamphlets, and the corresponding elements that should appear in the extent field.

4. Examples

Three Authors

Schramm, Wilbur ; Lyle, Jack ; Parker, Edwin B. – Television in the lives of our children. – Toronto : University of Toronto Press, c1961. – 324 p.

Four or More Authors

Boyd, Monica et al. – Ascription and achievement : studies in mobility and status attainment in Canada. – Ottawa : Carleton University Press, c1985. – 539 p. – (Carleton Library ; 133). – ISBN 0-88629-023-6

Collection with General Title

Lawrence, P. Scott. – Around the mulberry tree. – Toronto: Exile Editions, 1984. – 89 p. – Contents: The Malory Arms – When the elections came to town – Minutes of an evening – The mulberry tree – Conversation in the courtyard – Concerning the egg – Rondo – More conversations in the courtyard – Tea with Mrs Sharples – Ghosteps – Mood and rumor – Lunar observation. – ISBN 0-920428-79-7

SUMMARY OF EXTENT FIELD　　　　　　　　　　Illustration no. 9

Form	Elements to be entered	Example
A work in one volume	number of pages (expressed in Arabic numerals) and abbreviation for "page" (in lower case)	262 p.
A work in one volume with separately numbered parts	number of pages in each part and abbreviation for "page"	xxiii, 347 p. 52, 51 p.
A work in one volume with more than one pagination system for the parts	abbreviation for "multiple pagination"	Multiple pag.
Faulty pagination	number that appears on last page of the work, and brackets containing correction preceded by Latin abbreviation "i.e." ("that is")	278 [i.e., 287] p.
No pagination	pages are counted and total is recorded in brackets followed by the abbreviation for "page"	[232] p.
	or	
	estimated number of pages is recorded, preceded by abbreviation for "approximately"	Approx. 200 p.
Loose sheets	number of volumes and abbreviation for volume; parentheses containing abbreviation for "loose sheets" preceded by number	1 vol. (loose-leaf)
Several physical units	number of volumes and abbreviation for "volume" (in lower case)	3 vol.
Several physical units, publication continuing	three spaces followed by abbreviation for "volume"	▮▮▮vol.

Collection without General Title

One Author

Souster, Raymond. – The colour of the times. – Ten elephants on Yonge street. – Toronto : McGraw-Hill Ryerson, 1973. – 179 p. Originally published separately by Ryerson in 1964 and 1965. – ISBN 0-07-09275-0

Two Authors

Greenland, Caroline. – Ants. – Ivy, Bill. – Weasles. – [S.l.]: Grolier, c1985. – 47,47 p. – (Getting to know ... nature's children; 22). – ISBN 0-7172-1945-3 (Ants), ISBN 0-71721-913-5 (Weasels)

Work Coordinated by an Editor

Social problems : a Canadian profile. – Ed. Richard Laskin. – New York : McGraw-Hill, c1964. – 472 p.

Two Publishers

Virgilio, Nicholas A. – Selected haiku. – 2nd ed., augmented. – Sherbrooke : Burnt Lake Press ; Windsor, Ont. : Black Moss Press, 1988. – 78 p. – ISBN 0-920349-05-6 (Burnt Lake Press), ISBN 0-88753-180-6 (Black Moss Press)

Work with Several Subtitles

Segal, Gary L. – Immigrating to Canada : who is allowed? : what is required? : how to do it! – 6th ed. – Vancouver : International Self-Counsel Press, c1986. – 170 p. – (Self-Counsel Series). – ISBN 0-88908-625-5

Unpaginated Work

The Graphic work of Renoir : catalogue raisonné. – Compiled by Dr. Joseph G. Stella. – [S.l. : s.n., s.d.]. – [111] p.

5. Book Part

Book parts may be chapters or sections of a book, essays or articles grouped together on the basis of a common feature, such as author, theme or subject, or stories or poems gathered into a collection. Other variations and combinations are often found.

An entry for a book part, as opposed to a complete book, should contain the following information, in accordance with the entry outline for a document part, described in Rule 4:

- the author's name
- the title of the part, enclosed in angle quotes, in accordance with Rule 68
- all the bibliographic information for the host document, including the ISBN (the ISBN number is a direct and reliable access point in an automated database and at the same time is a control mechanism for positive identification of the host document)
- location of the part in the host document (i.e., the first and last pages on which the part appears). The location in the host document is indicated by the abbreviation "P." for "page" (capitalized because it opens the field), followed by the page number(s) (in Arabic numerals). Consecutive page numbers are separated by an en dash without spaces (e.g., P. 17-32), whereas discontinuous page numbers are separated by a comma (e.g., P. 20, 66). Note that entries for multivolume works should include the volume number(s), indicated by the abbreviation "Vol." (capitalized because it opens the field), followed by an Arabic numeral and separated from the page reference by a comma (e.g., Vol. 2, p. 125-157).

6. Examples

All Parts by One Author

MacLennan, Hugh. – «Part eight : Conrad Dehmel's story as told by himself». – Voices in time. – Toronto : Macmillan, c1980. – ISBN 0-7715-9570-0. – P. 250-259

Each Part by a Different Author

The entry is created under the name of the author of the part. The name of the editor, if any, is entered in the secondary author field.

> Frye, Northrop. – «Haliburton : Mask & Ego». – Beginnings : a critical anthology.
> – Ed. John Moss. – Toronto : New Canada Publications, c1980. – (The
> Canadian Novel ; 2). – ISBN 0-919601-05-7. – P. 40-44

Encyclopedia or Dictionary Article

The entry is created under the author's name if known. Otherwise, it is listed under the title of the article. (Note: An article in a standard reference work will often have a set of initials as a signature. Generally, an author so designated can be identified from the list of contributors, usually given at the beginning of the reference work.)

> Whiteley, William H. – «Duckworth, Sir John Thomas». – Dictionary of
> Canadian Biography. – Toronto: University of Toronto Press ; Québec: Presse
> de l'Université Laval, 1983. – ISBN 0-8020-3398-9. – Vol. 5, p. 273-275

> «Veterinary Science». – Encyclopedia Canadiana. – Toronto : Grolier, c1975.
> – ISBN 0-7172-1602-0

Section with Several Parts, All by the Same Author

The section title, when there is one, is recorded in the entry in the same way as a chapter title. The individual titles of parts are given in a note.

> Moisan, Clément. – «4. Poetry of clandestiny». – A poetry of frontiers :
> comparative studies in Quebec/Canadian literature. – Victoria : Press Porcépic,
> c1983. – (Three Solitudes, contemporary literary criticism in Canada ; 5). –
> Contents: *Alain Grandbois* - Earle Birney, *Hector de Saint-Denys Garneau* -
> John Glassco, *Anne Hébert* - P.K. Page, *Rina Lasnier* - Margaret Avison. –
> Translation of *Poésie des frontières*. – ISBN 0-88878-078-8. – P. 49-75

Section with Several Parts, Each by a Different Author

The entry is created under the section title; the titles of the part and the names of the authors are given in a note.

> «III. Major systems and processes of Canadian society. D. Control and
> deviance». – Sociology Canada : readings. – Edited by C. Beattie, S. Crysdale.
> – Toronto : Butterworth, c1974. – Includes «Socialization in prison» by W.E.
> Mann, «Social class and bar behaviour during the Calgary Stampede» by
> Richard J. Ossenberg, «Drug use among students» by Paul C. Whitehead and
> Reginald G. Smart. – ISBN 0-409-81326-5. – P. 364-393

Section 2
Braille and Large-Print Documents

An entry for a braille or large-print document contains the fields and elements shown in Illustration no. 10. The field numbers are those described in the general entry outline in Rule 3.

1. Scope

This section covers documents produced in a format that can be read by the visually impaired. Large-print documents use character sizes ranging from 18 to 24 points, whereas most other documents use character sizes ranging from 10 to 12 points. braille uses raised dots to represent a conventional alphabet, thereby allowing the visually handicapped to read a document by touch.

2. Bibliographic Information Source

The information required to create a bibliographic entry for a braille or large-print document usually appears on the work's title page or title page verso. Some information may also appear on the cover or in the printer's imprint at the back of the publication. If these sources do not list all the bibliographic information, it should be obtained from reference works and enclosed in brackets, in accordance with Rule 11.

3. Special Bibliographic Features

Entries for braille or large-print documents follow the same conventions as for book or serial entries, except that a descriptive identifier ("braille" or "large print") is included in the title field. It is expressed in lower case and enclosed in brackets immediately after the title or alternative title, in accordance with Rule 64.

Information about the technical nature of the work (e.g., the size of large print or the system of braille) or about the edition of the work used for the braille or large-print version may be given in a note.

ENTRY OUTLINE FOR BRAILLE
OR LARGE-PRINT DOCUMENTS

No.	FIELD	ELEMENTS	
		Book	**Serial**
1.	Author Personal or corporate name. –	Mowat, Farley. –	Selected articles from Reader's Digest [large print]. –
2.	Title Title alternative title [descriptive identifier] : subtitle = parallel title. –	Never cry wolf [large print]. –	
3.	Seconday authors Name of translator, illustrator, editor. –		
4.	Edition Number, descriptor. –		
5.	In the case of serial: Issue designation Volume, number (date). –		(July 1976)- .–
6.	Publication data Place: publisher, date.–	Thorndike, Maine: Thorndike Press, [1982]. –	Mt. Morris, Ill. : Reader's Digest Association, 1976- .–
7.	Extent Number of pages or volumes. –	242 p. –	vol. –
8.	Series (Title ; numbering). –		
9.	Notes Additional information. –	Original edition published in 1963. –	Monthly. –
10.	Standard numbers ISBN and ISSN	ISBN 0-89621-402-8	ISSN 0163-6405

Book

Mowat, Farley. – Never cry wolf [large print]. – Thorndike, Maine : Thorndike Press, [1982]. – 242 p. – Original edition published in 1963. – ISBN 0-89621-402-8

Serial Publication

Selected articles from Reader's Digest [large print]. – (July 1976)-   . – Mt. Morris, Ill. : Reader's Digest Association, 1976-   . – vol. – Monthly. – ISSN 0163-6405

Section 3
Machine-Readable Records

An entry for a machine-readable record contains the fields and elements shown in Illustration no. 11. The field numbers are those described in the general entry outline in Rule 3.

1. Scope

This section establishes the conventions for bibliographic entries for machine-readable records. A machine-readable record is information contained in a format that can be read and interpreted only with the aid of a machine (usually a computer). Machine-readable formats include magnetic tapes, diskettes and CD-ROM. This section covers only the conventions for the bibliographic description of diskettes (i.e., software used for storing data).

2. Bibliographic Information Source

Bibliographic entries for machine-readable records are based on the information that appears on the label of the diskette. When there is no label on the diskette, information is taken from any accompanying documentation or from the diskette envelope or container. If these sources do not list all the bibliographic information, it may be obtained from documentation related to the file (e.g., from producers, distributors, or reviews in magazines). Any information taken from sources outside the document should be enclosed in brackets, in accordance with Rule 11.

3. Special Bibliographic Features

The entry for a machine-readable record is usually created under the title. The title field contains the descriptive identifier "machine-readable record", expressed in lower case and in the singular, and enclosed in brackets, immediately after the title or alternative title, in accordance with Rule 64.

ENTRY OUTLINE FOR MACHINE-READABLE RECORDS　　　　*Illustration no. 11*

No. FIELD	ELEMENTS
2. Title Title alternative title [descriptive identifier] : subtitle = parallel title. –	Alexander-Plus Telex I [machine- readable record]. –
3. Secondary authors Name of producer, sponsoring organization. –	
4. Edition Version. –	
6. Publication data Place : publisher, date. –	Hull: Corporation Omzig, [s.-d.].–
7. Extent Number of physical units. –	2 disks. –
8. Series (Title ; numbering). –	
9. Notes Additional information	Requires IBM PC or compatible, 256K, MS DOS/PC-DOS, 2 disk drives, Hayes modern compatible; hard disk recommended

Alexander - Plus Telex I [machine readable record]. – Hull: Corporation Omzig, [s.d.]. – 2 disks. – Requires IBM PC or compatible, 256K, MS DOS/PC-DOS, 2 disk drives, Hayes modem compatible; hard disk recommended

The secondary author field contains the names of persons who participated in some capacity in the production of the document (e.g., the programmer).

The edition field indicates the software version number.

The extent field cites the number of physical units that make up the document, followed by a document descriptor (e.g., 2 diskettes).

The notes field provides the following information:

- the document title if the document is available in another language and the title may be easily ascertained
- the distributor's name and address if the document is not easily accessible
- the presence of any accompanying document (e.g., a user's guide)
- the type of equipment required to use the document.

4. Example

Document available in another language

Communiqué [machine-readable record]. – Version 3.0. – Nepean, Ont. : Pelada Informatica, c1986. – Requires DOS of 2.0 or higher, 640k RAM, hard disc. – French version with same name

Section 4
Manuscripts

A bibliographic entry for a manuscript contains the fields and elements shown in Illustration no. 12. The field numbers are those described in the general entry outline in Rule 3.

1. Scope

This section provides guidelines for creating a bibliographic entry for a handwritten or typed manuscript. A manuscript is usually a draft that is preliminary to the final, commercially printed version of the work. As a manuscript is unpublished, a bibliographic entry for such a work has several notable differences from an entry for a published work, as indicated by the following guidelines.

2. Bibliographic Information Source

Bibliographic information for a manuscript is taken directly from the document. Any information taken from other sources should be enclosed in brackets, in accordance with Rule 11.

3. Special Bibliographic Features

Information should be recorded exactly as it is found in the source since unusual usage (e.g., spelling or punctuation) may be employed by the author for a particular purpose. If changes are made when the information is transcribed (e.g., for the purpose of clarity), the nature of the changes and the reason for them should be indicated in a note.

The various drafts or versions are listed in the edition field.

The publication data field contains only the date that the document was produced.

The notes field may provide the following information:

- the type of manuscript (handwritten, typed or photocopied)
- the location where it was produced, if known
- the name(s) of the contributor(s)
- publication data, if the work was published

ENTRY OUTLINE FOR MANUSCRIPTS   *Illustration no. 12*

No. FIELD	**ELEMENTS**
1. Author Personal name. –	Smart, Elizabeth. –

2.   Title
      Title alternative
      title : subtitle. –
	[Notebook]. –

3.   Secondary authors
      Name of illustrator,
      etc. –	

4. Edition Draft or version. –	
5. Publication data Date only. –	October 17, 1939-August 30, 1940. –
7. Extent Number of physical units. –	18 p. –

9.   Notes
      Additional
      information
	Contents: «Mexico trying to translate Alice Paalen's poems, French vocabulary, etc. A dream of G.B. before I met him; a few poems». – National Library of Canada Manuscripts Collection, Elizabeth Smart Papers, MSS 1983-5/1987-9, Series B.1, box 3, f9

Smart, Elizabeth. – [Notebook]. – October 17, 1939-August 30, 1940. – 18 p. – Contents: «Mexico trying to translate Alice Paalen's poems, French vocabulary, etc. A dream of G.B. before I met him; a few poems». – National Library of Canada Manuscripts Collection, Elizabeth Smart Papers, MSS 1983-5/1987-9, Series B.1, box 3, f9

- restrictions on the manuscript (e.g., limited consultation until a certain date)
- the name and location of the repository

4. *Example*

Letter

Pellan, Alfred. – [Letter to Jordy Dumas on the subject of mural painting]. – 18 [January] 1983. – 2 sheets. – Private collection

Buchan, John. – [Letter to Arthur Murray, describing a visit by Buchan to Washington]. – 3rd April 1937. – 1 sheet. – Kingston : Queen's University Archives. – Written at Government House, Ottawa

Section 5
Maps and Atlases

Maps

The entry for a map should contain the fields and elements shown in Illustration no. 13. The field numbers are those described in the general entry outline in Rule 3.

1. Scope

The following rules establish the conventions for bibliographic entries for maps as independent works. The conventions for maps published in a larger work (e.g., a book, periodical or microfiche) are the same as those for a host document. Sample entries for maps published in larger documents are given in Section 5 ("Map Reproductions") below.

2. Bibliographic Information Source

The bibliographic information is taken from the map itself. Some information may also appear on the wrapper or container, or on documentation accompanying the map. If these sources do not list all the bibliographic information, it should be obtained from reference works and enclosed in brackets, in accordance with Rule 11.

3. Special Bibliographic Features

Entries for maps are usually created under the name of the corporate body issuing the map. If the name of the cartographer is cited, it appears in the secondary authors field.

ENTRY OUTLINE FOR MAPS

No. FIELD	ELEMENTS
1. Author	Canada. Survey and Mapping Branch. –
Name of corporate body or individual. –	
2. Title	Ottawa : Ontario, Quebec. –
Title alternative title : sub-title = parallel title. –	
3. Secondary authors	
Name of any person or corporate body associated with the production of the map. –	
4. Edition	10th ed. –
Number descriptor. –	
6. Publication data	Ottawa : the Branch, 1983. –
Place : publisher, date. –	
7. Extent	1 map. –
Number of physical units. –	
8. Series	
(Title ; numbering). –	
9. Notes	Scale, 1:50 000. – Based on photographs
Additional information	taken in 1984. – Reference no. 31G/5

Canada. Surveys and Mapping Branch. – Ottawa : Ontario, Quebec. – 10th ed. – Ottawa : the Branch, c1987. – 1 map. – Scale, 1:50 000. – Based on photographs taken in 1984. – Reference no. 31G/5

The extent field lists the number of physical units that make up the document, and a document descriptor (e.g., 2 maps). A map as an independent work can be published in one of various formats, which should be noted by one of the following expressions:

Physical description	Descriptor
one map on a single sheet	1 map
one map on several sheets	1 map in 4 sections
several maps on a single sheet	3 maps on 1 sheet

The notes field lists the scale of the map (i.e., the ratio between actual distance and the size of the map).

4. Example

Several Maps on a Single Sheet

Canada. Surveys and Mapping Branch. – Territorial evolution of Canada. – 2nd ed. – Ottawa : the Branch, 1969. – 23 maps on 1 sheet. – Scale, 1:50 500 000. – Reference no. MCR 2306

5. Map Reproductions

A bibliographic entry for a map published in a larger document follows the general entry outline for a document part, as given in Rule 4 ("Part of a Document"), and includes the following information:

- the author name and the map title (enclosed in quotation marks), according to Rule 68 ("Title of a Document Part"), and
- all the information regarding the document in which the map is published (e.g., a book, periodical, slide or microfiche).

If available, information about the scale of the map is listed at the beginning of the notes field.

6. Examples

Map Published in an Atlas

«Stages in the last delaciation [sic] of northern Canada». – Canada's north : the reference manual. – Ottawa : Communications Branch, Indian and Northern Affairs Canada, 1983. – French title: Le Nord canadien. – Cat. no. R71-31/1983E. – ISBN 0-660-11483-6. – P. 2-20

Map Published in a Bilingual Atlas

The entry below follows the conventions for describing an atlas and for identifying a bilingual document (see Chapter 6).

Desceliers, Pierre. – «La Nouvelle-France en 1550 = New France in 1550». – Atlas de la Nouvelle-France = An atlas of New France. – Compiled by Marcel Trudel. – [Quebec] : Les Presses de l'université Laval, 1968. – Side-by-side texts in English and French. – Original held by National Archives of Canada. – P. 54

Map in a periodical

«Vancouver : location of homes and businesses of Japanese and Chinese immigrants». – The Canadian geographer = Le Géographe canadien. – Vol. 32, no. 4 (Winter 1988). – ISSN 00083658. – P. 358

Map on a Slide

«Ontario : geological regions» [slide]. – Ontario in maps. – Conceived and written by Len Swatridge. – Toronto : McIntyre Educational Media, c1983. – (Regional geography of Canada, an economic and urban study ; 330500). – Slide no. 62. Atlases

Atlas

The entry for an atlas contains the fields and elements shown in Illustration no. 14. The field numbers are those described in the general outline in Rule 3.

1. Scope

The following rules establish the conventions for compiling bibliographic entries for atlases.

2. Bibliographic Information Source

The information required to create a bibliographic entry for an atlas is usually found on the document's title page or title page verso. Some information elements (e.g., a series title) may also appear on the cover or dust jacket. If these sources do not list all the bibliographic information, it should be obtained from reference works and enclosed in brackets, in accordance with Rule 11.

3. Special Bibliographic Features

Entries for atlases follow the same conventions that pertain to book entries, except that the extent field lists the number of atlases, rather than the number of pages or volumes. If the atlas is in two or more languages, the conventions for bilingual documents also apply (see Chapter 6).

4. Examples

Atlas in Two Languages

Rolph-McNally Limited. – Road atlas Canada USA = Atlas routier Canada USA. – [Downsview, Ont.] : Rolph-McNally, [s.d.]. – 1 atlas. – Text in English and French

Dudycha, Douglas J. et al. – The Canadian atlas of recreation and exercise = L'atlas canadien de la récréation et de l'activité physique. – Waterloo, Ont. : Dept. of Geography, University of Waterloo, 1983. – 1 atlas. – (Department of Geography Publication Series ; no. 21). – English and French text in parallel columns

No. FIELD	ELEMENTS
1. Author Corporate or personal name. –	Kerr, D.G.G. –
2. Title Title alternative title : subtitle = parallel title. –	Historical atlas of Canada. –
3. Secondary authors Names of persons or corporate bodies involved in the production of the atlas. –	
4. Edition Number descriptor. –	3rd rev. ed. –
6. Publication data Place : publisher, date. –	Don Mills, Ont.: Thomas Nelson & Sons (Canada), 1975. –
7. Extent Number of atlases. –	1 atlas. –
8. Series (Title ; numbering). –	
9. Notes Additional information. –	
10. Standard number ISBN	ISBN 0-176-00409-2

Kerr, D.G.G. – Historical atlas of Canada. – 3rd rev. ed. – Don Mills, Ont. :
Thomas Nelson & Sons (Canada), 1975. – 1 atlas. – ISBN 0-176-00409-2

Section 6
Microforms

A bibliographic entry for a microfiche or microfilm contains the fields and elements shown in Illustration no. 15. The field numbers are those described in the general entry outline in Rule 3.

1. Scope

This section establishes the conventions for the bibliographic description of microforms (i.e., microfiches and microfilms). The conventions for part of a microform are discussed in part 5 of this section ("Microform Part").

2. Bibliographic Information Source

Bibliographic information for a microform is usually found on the first or last frame of the document. Some information may appear on the wrapper or container, the accompanying documentation, or the top edge of a microfiche. If these sources do not list all the required information, it may be obtained from reference works, in which case it should be enclosed in brackets, in accordance with Rule 11.

3. Special Bibliographic Features

An entry for a microform should provide information about both the medium (i.e., the microform) and the nature of the work reproduced on the microform. Consequently the record will include bibliographic information specific to the microform and bibliographic information specific to the document reproduced, such as the issue designation in the case of a periodical. All information about the original document may be given in a note.

The title field contains the descriptive identifier "microform", regardless of whether the document is a microfiche or a microfilm. The descriptive identifier, enclosed in brackets and expressed in lower case and in the singular, appears immediately after the title or alternative title, as specified in Rule 64.

ENTRY OUTLINE FOR MICROFICHES AND MICROFILMS

No. FIELD	ELEMENTS	
	Microfiche	**Microfilm**
1. Author Personal or corporate name. –	Traill, Catherine Parr. –	Moodie, Susanna. –
2. Title Title alternative title [descriptive identifier] : subtitle = parallel title. –	The backwoods of Canada [microform] : being letters from the wife of an emigrant officer ... –	Life in the backwoods, a sequel to Roughing it in the bush [microform]. –
3. Secondary authors Names of persons or organizations involved in producing the document. –		
6. Publication data Place : publisher, date. –	[Ottawa] : Canadian Institute for Historical Microreproductions, [s.d.]. –	Cambridge, Mass. : General Microfilm, [s.d.]. –
7. Extent Number and type of microforms. –	4 microfiches. –	1 reel of microfilm. –
8. Series (Title ; numbering). –		
9. Notes Additional information. –	Originally published in London, 1836. – CIHM edition no. 41930. –	Originally published in New York by John W. Lovell, 1887
10. Standard number ISBN	ISBN 0-665-41930-9	

Microfiche

Traill, Catherine Parr. – The backwoods of Canada [microform] : being letters from the wife of an emigrant officer . . . – [Ottawa] : Canadian Institute for Historical Microreproductions, [s.d.]. – 4 microfiches. – Originally published in London, 1836. – CIHM edition no. 41930. – ISBN 0-665-41930-9

Microfilm

Moodie, Susanna. – Life in the backwoods, a sequel to Roughing it in the bush [microform]. – Cambridge, Mass. : General Microfilm, [s.d.]. – 1 reel of microfilm. – Originally published in New York by John W. Lovell, 1887

Note: The contents of an entry for a microform will depend on the type of document reproduced. For instance, an entry for a serial publication will contain an issue designation field (see "Special Bibliographic Features" below).

The issue designation refers to the serial publication reproduced on microform.

The publication data field contains publishing information about the microform; the place of publication, publisher, and date of publication of the original work can be listed in a note.

The extent field indicates the number of physical units and the document descriptor (e.g., 5 microfiches or 2 microfilms). For a microform series that is still being published, the number of physical units is replaced by three spaces before the descriptor (see Rule 112).

The notes field provides the following information, when appropriate:

- the abbreviation "col." if the microform is in colour
- whether the microform is available in other formats
- details about the original document (e.g., publication data).

4. Examples

A Thesis Manuscript on Microfiche

Norman, Joanne S. – The psychomachia in medieval art [microform] : metamorphoses of an allegory. – Ottawa : National Library of Canada, 1980. – 4 microfiches. – (Canadian Theses on Microfiche). – Ph.D. thesis, University of Ottawa, 1979

A Periodical on Microfilm

Saturday night [microform]. – Vol. 88, no. 1 (January 1973)-vol. 90, no. 7 (December 1975). – Toronto : Micromedia, 1976. – 1 reel. – ISSN 0036-4975

5. Microform Part

Like an entry for a complete microform, an entry for a microform part should contain bibliographic information about both the microform and the reproduced work (e.g., the issue designation for a periodical and the location of the part in the reproduced periodical).

In accordance with the general entry outline for a document part, described in Rule 4, an entry for a microform part should contain the following information:

- the author's name
- the title of the part, enclosed in quotation marks (see Rule 68 ("Title of Document Part")
- information about the host document (i.e., the microfiche or microfilm), including the standard number
- the location of the part in the reproduced work, and on the microform if the host document consists of several physical units. In the latter case, the term "Microfiche" (or "Reel" for a microfilm) is entered, followed by the number of the microfiche or reel. The term is capitalized, as it opens the field (e.g., Reel 17).

6. *Example*

Newspaper Article on Microfilm

Platiel, Rudy. – [Indian in the North should control own health care system, report says]. – The Globe and Mail [microform]. – June 9, 1984. – P. A5. – ISSN 0319-0714

Section 7
Motion Pictures and Video Recordings

A bibliographic entry for a motion picture or a video recording contains the fields and elements shown in Illustration no. 16. The field numbers are those described in the general outline in Rule 3.

1. Scope

This section establishes the conventions for bibliographic entries for motion pictures and video recordings.

2. Bibliographic Information Source

The bibliographic information for a motion picture or a video recording is taken from the credits, which are found at the beginning or at the end of the document and list the names of directors, producers, actors and other persons who contributed to the production of the document. Some information may also appear on the wrapper or on accompanying documentation. If these sources do not list all the needed information, it may be obtained from reference works, in which case it should be enclosed in brackets, in accordance with Rule 11.

3. Special Bibliographic Features

An entry for a motion picture or video recording is usually listed under the title (see Rule 51). The title field contains the descriptive identifier "motion picture" or "video recording". The descriptive identifier is expressed in lower case and in the singular, and is enclosed in brackets, immediately after the title or alternative title, in accordance with Rule 64.

Illustration no. 16   ***ENTRY OUTLINE FOR MOTION PICTURES AND VIDEO RECORDINGS***

No. FIELD	ELEMENTS	
	Film	**Video**
2. Title Title alternative title [descriptive identifier] : subtitle = parallel title. –	A night stop [motion picture]. –	The Psychomachia by Prudentius [video recording]. –
3. Secondary authors Name of producer, sponsoring agency. –	Producer, Robert Holbrook. –	Producer, Malcolm Cobley. –
6. Publication data Place : production company, date. –	Ottawa : Algonquin College, Technology and Trades Division, Film Production, 1979. –	Toronto : Media Centre for Medieval Studies, University of Toronto, [1978?]. –
7. Extent Number of physical units, running time, film size. –	1 reel, 19 min., 16 mm. –	1 cassette, 22 min., 3/4 in. –
8. Series (Title ; numbering). –		
9. Notes Additional information	Col.	Col.

Motion Picture

A night stop [motion picture]. – Producer, Robert Holbrook. – Ottawa : Algonquin College, Technology and Trades Division, Film Production, 1979. – 1 reel, 19 min., 16 mm. – Col.

Video Recording

The Psychomachia by Prudentius [video recording]. – Producer, Malcolm Cobley. – Toronto : Media Centre, Centre for Medieval Studies, University of Toronto, [1978?]. – 1 cassette, 22 min., 3/4 in. – Col.

The secondary author field contains the names and role descriptions of persons who participated in some capacity in the production of the work (e.g., director, producer, cameraman). The secondary author field also contains the name of the sponsoring organization. Note that, as the list of secondary authors can become quite extensive, this field should be limited to the names of persons whose contribution to the production of the film was substantial or whose names are important for bibliographic purposes. The cast may be listed in a note.

The extent field contains the following information:
- the number of physical units that make up the document, followed by a document descriptor (i.e., the number of film reels or video cassettes)
- the running time (in minutes)
- the width of the medium (in millimetres for films and inches for video recordings).

These elements of information are separated by commas.

The notes field lists:
- the document title if the document is available in another language and that information is easily accessible
- whether the version in question contains subtitles or captions for the hearing-impaired
- the cast (i.e, actors, moderators and participants)
- the distributor's name and address if the document is not easily accessible
- whether the document is in colour, in black and white, or partly in colour and partly in black and white (the abbreviations "b&w" and "col." are recommended)
- the presence of any accompanying document (e.g., a pamphlet or poster)
- whether the document is available in other forms
- the trademark for a video recording (e.g., VHS, BETA or Philips VCR), as this information indicates the type of equipment required for use of the document.

4. Examples

Document Available in Another Language

Democracy, leadership, commitment [video]. – Produced by Mick Jackson. – Toronto : Ontario Educational Communications Authority, [1980?]. – 1 cassette, 57 min., 3/4 in. – (The age of uncertainty). – Edited and narrated by John Kenneth Galbraith. – Col. – French title: Démocratie, autorité, face à l'avenir

Information about the Cast

Mon oncle Antoine [motion picture]. – Director Claude Jutra, script by Clément Perron, photography by Michel Brault. – [Montreal] : National Film Board of Canada, c1971. – 4 reels, 110 min, 16 mm. – French version available with same title. – Cast: Jean Duceppe, Olivette Thibault, Claude Jutra, Hélène Loiselle, Lionel Villeneuve, Monique Mercure, Jacques Gagnon, Lyne Champagne. – Col. – Also available in 35 mm and video cassette. – NFB cat. no. 1 10171 003

Entry for a Series

The series title is entered in the title field, and the component documents of the series are listed in the notes field, in accordance with Rule 69.

> The age of uncertainty [video]. – Toronto : Ontario Educational Communications Authority, [1980?]. – 15 cassettes, 57 min. each, 3/4 in. – Edited and narrated by John Kenneth Galbraith. – Col. – Names of parts: The prophets and promise of classical capitalism, Manners and morals of high capitalism, Karl Marx and direct dissent, The colonial idea, Lenin and the great ungluing, The rise and fall of money, The mandarin revolution, The fatal competition, The big corporation, Land and the people, The metropolis, Democracy, leadership, commitment, Weekend in Vermont (3 cassettes). – French title: Le temps des incertitudes

In an entry for only one part of a series, the title of the part appears in the title field, and the general title of the series is given in the series field, in accordance with Rule 116.

> Democracy, leadership, commitment [video]. – Produced by Mick Jackson. – Toronto : Ontario Educational Communications Authority, [1980?]. – 1 cassette, 57 min., 3/4 in. – (The age of uncertainty). – Edited and narrated by John Kenneth Galbraith. – Col. – French title: Démocratie, autorité, face à l'avenir

Section 8
Multimedia Kits

An entry for a multimedia kit contains the fields and elements shown in Illustration no. 17. The field numbers are those described in the general entry outline in Rule 3.

1. Scope

This section provides guidelines on bibliographic entries for multimedia kits. A multimedia kit is a combination of any two or more materials produced in several media (e.g., a story presented partially as a book and partially as a recording, packaged as a unit).

2. Bibliographic Information Source

The bibliographic information for multimedia kits is taken from the label on the wrapper or container. If there is no wrapper, the entry is created on the basis of the bibliographic information source that gives the most information. If these sources do not provide all the necessary information, it may be taken from reference works, in which case it should be enclosed in brackets, in accordance with Rule 11.

3. Special Bibliographic Features

The title field contains the descriptive identifier "multimedia kit", expressed in lower case and in the singular and enclosed in brackets immediately after the title or alternative title, in accordance with Rule 64.

The extent field lists all the documents that make up the kit (e.g., 2 posters, 1 cassette, 40 slides).

ENTRY OUTLINE FOR MULTIMEDIA KITS

No. FIELD	ELEMENTS
1. Author Personal or corporate name. –	Spyri, Johanna. –
2. Title Title alternative title [descriptive identifier] : subtitle = parallel title. –	Heidi [multimedia kit]. –
3. Secondary authors Name of designer, scriptwriter, graphic artist, sponsoring agency. –	Read by Petula Clark. –
6. Publication data Place : publisher, date. –	Don Mills, Ont. : ALS Audio Language Studies, [1986]. –
7. Extent Numbers and descriptor. –	2 cassettes, 1 book. –
8. Series (Title ; numbering). –	(Read-along ; 7109-7). –
9. Notes Additional information. –	Arranged for recording by J. Dunn. –
10 Standard number ISBN	ISBN 0-88646-813-2

Spyri, Johanna. – Heidi [multimedia kit]. – Read by Petula Clark. – Don Mills,
Ont. : ALS Audio Language Studies, [1986]. – 2 cassettes, 1 book. –
(Read-along ; 7109-7). – Arranged for recording by J. Dunn. – ISBN
0886468132

4. Examples

An introduction to office technology [multimedia kit]. – Text by Margaret
McKelvey. – Toronto : Mead Sound Filmstrips, c1982. – 4 cassettes, 1 brochure,
4 filmstrips. – (Series ; 83). – Also available in French, entitled Le travail au
bureau

January 15th 1910 [multimedia kit]. – Toronto : Gage Educational Publishing,
c1971. – 1 disc, 8 boxes of booklets and printed reproductions of everyday items
from 1910

Regional geography of Canada [multimedia kit] : an economic and urban study.
– Toronto : McIntyre Educational Media, c1978. – 1 cassette, 1 filmstrip, 50
slides, 3 overhead transparencies. – (Curriculum Studies in Geography for
Canadian Schools). – Publisher's reference: MEU, The Atlantic Provinces

Take me along [multimedia kit]. – Ottawa : NOVALIS, c1970. – 1 cassette, 30
slides, 1 booklet

Section 9
Photographs

A bibliographic entry for a photograph contains the fields and elements shown in Illustration no. 18. The field numbers are those described in the general entry outline in Rule 3.

1. Scope

This section provides guidelines for the bibliographic description of photographs, whether original works or reproductions.

2. Bibliographic Information Source

Bibliographic information for a photograph is taken from the document itself, from documentation provided by the owner of the photograph or from reference works. If information is taken from sources other than the document, it should be enclosed in brackets, in accordance with Rule 11.

3. Special Bibliographic Features

The publication data field contains only the date of the work's creation.

The extent field gives the document's dimensions (i.e., height and width). The frame or mounting size are not included in the dimensions.

The notes field provides the following information:

- whether the photograph is in colour or in black and white (use of the abbreviations "col." and "b&w" is recommended)
- the process used to produce the photograph
- the repository.

No. FIELD	ELEMENTS
1. Author Photographer's name. –	Cartier-Bresson, Henri. –
2. Title Title alternative title : subtitle = parallel title. –	Martigues, France 1932-33. –
6. Publication data Only the date of creation. –	[1933?]. –
7. Extent Dimensions. –	24.8 x 16.1 cm. –
9. Notes Additional information	B&w. -- Gelatin-silver print. – Museum of Modern Art, New York

Cartier-Bresson, Henri. – Martigues, France 1932-33. – [1933?]. – 24.8 x 16.1 cm. – B&w. – Gelatin-silver print. – Museum of Modern Art, New York

4. Examples

Reproductions

An entry for a reproduction of a photograph should list the following information: the photographer's name, the title of the reproduced photograph, in quotation marks as specified in Rule 68, and details about the reproduction's location (e.g., book, periodical, set of slides, or microfiche). Any available information about the original photograph is given in a note.

Reproduction In a Book

Gutmann, John. – «San Francisco celebrates the opening of World's Fair». – Sutnik, Maia-Mari. – Gutmann. – Toronto : Art Gallery of Ontario, c1985. – 26.7 x 30.8 cm; from the collection of the artist, courtesy Fraenkel Gallery, San Francisco. – ISBN 0-919777-18-X. – Plate 56

Reproduction In a Periodical

Adams, Ansel. – «Mount Williamson, the Sierra Nevada, from Marzanar, California». – ARTnews. – Vol. 88, no. 4 (April 1989). – ISSN 0004-3273. – P. 168-169

Section 10
Printed Music

Bibliographic entries for printed music contain the fields and elements shown in Illustration no. 19. The field numbers are those described in the general entry outline in Rule 3.

1. Scope

This section provides guidelines on entries for works of printed music, such as a full score (i.e., a work in which all the instrumental and vocal parts appear on a series of staves vertically aligned) or a particular kind of score (e.g., a vocal score or piano score).

2. Bibliographic Information Source

The information required to create an entry for a work of printed music is usually found on the document's title page or title page verso. Some information may also appear on the cover or the printer's imprint at the back of the publication. If these sources do not list all the bibliographic information, it may be obtained from reference works, in which case it should be enclosed in brackets, in accordance with Rule 11.

3. Special Bibliographic Features

Entries for works of printed music follow the same conventions as those for books, except for the addition of the descriptive identifier "music". It should be expressed in lower case and enclosed in brackets, immediately after the title or alternative title, in accordance with Rule 64. Secondary information, such as the publisher's order number or the plate number, is listed in the notes field. A plate number identifies a specific edition of a work and may be useful in dating an undated music publication.

No. FIELD	ELEMENTS
1. Author Composer's name. –	Garant, Serge. –
2. Title Title alternative title [descriptive identifier] : subtitle = parallel title. –	Pièce pour piano, no 2 (Cage d'oiseau) [music]. –
3. Secondary authors Name of songwriter, arranger, adapter. –	
4. Edition Number descriptor. –	
6. Publication data Place : publisher, date. –	Don Mills (Ont.) : BMI Canada, c1969. –
7. Extent Number of pages. –	8 p. –
8. Series (Title ; numbering). –	(Music of the Nineteen Sixties and after)
9. Notes Additional information (e.g., plate number or publisher's order number)	

Garant, Serge. – Pièce pour piano, n° 2 (Cage d'oiseau) [music]. – Don Mills (Ont.) : BMI Canada, c1969. – 8 p. – (Music of the Nineteen Sixties and after)

4. Examples

Anka, Paul ; Carson, Johnny. – Johnny's theme [music]. – Arranged by Roger Pemberton. – Winona, Minn. : Hal Leonard Publishing, c1965. – (Intermediate Jazz Ensemble Series). – Publisher's reference no. : 00807300

Clerc, Julien. – Coeur de rocker [music]. – Paroles de Luc Plamondon. – Mont St-Hilaire: Chant de mon pays, c1984. – 6 p. – Edition no.: CD 147

Morel, François. – Quatuor à cordes n° 2 [music]. – Toronto : Berandol Music, c1982. – 30 p. – Edition no.: BER 1851

Raineri, G. – The Dufferin galop, op. 50. – Halifax : J.P. Hagarty Musical Warehouse, c1873. – [5] p. – Dedicated to Mrs. Col. Gordon. – Composed on the occasion of Lord and Lady Dufferin's visit to Halifax, 1873

Section 11
Serials and Serial Parts

Illustration no. 20 lists the various elements that should appear in an entry for a serial run. Because of the variations among different kinds of serials, two examples are presented: a magazine and an annual report. The field numbers are those described in the general entry outline in Rule 3.

1. Scope

Anglo-American cataloguing rules, second edition, defines a serial as a "publication in any medium issued in successive parts bearing numerical or chronological designations and intended to be continued indefinitely. Serials include periodicals; newspapers; annuals (reports, yearbooks, etc.); the journals, memoirs, proceedings, transactions, etc., of societies; and numbered monographic series" (p. 570). This section establishes the conventions for the bibliographic description of a complete or partial run of a serial publication. Part 5 specifies the rules governing entries for a single serial issue, and Part 7 describes the rules for an article in a periodical.

2. Bibliographic Information Source

Bibliographic information for a serial publication is usually taken from the title page or title page verso. Some information may also appear on the cover. If these sources do not list all the required information, it may be taken from reference works or publishers' catalogues, in which case it should be enclosed in brackets, in accordance with Rule 11.

Entries for serial runs are generally less common than entries for serial parts. Creating entries for serial runs may also be more complex and difficult. Inconsistencies may appear from issue to issue of the serial or even within a single issue.

3. Special Bibliographic Features

Entries for serial runs are generally less common than entries for serial parts. Creating entries for serial runs may also be more complex and difficult. Inconsistencies may appear from issue to issue of the serial or even within a single issue.

No.	FIELD	ELEMENTS	
		Periodical	**Annual report**
1.	Author Personal or corporate name. –	Writers Guild of Alberta. –	National Energy Board. –
2.	Title Title alternative title : subtitle = parallel title. –	Newsletter. –	Annual report. –
3.	Secondary author Name of the Sponsoring body.–		
4.	Edition Descriptive expression. –		
5.	Issue designation Volume, number (date)- . –	Vol. 1, no. 1 (Dec. 1980)- .–	(1959) - . –
6.	Publication data Place : publisher, date. –	Edmonton : the Guild, 1980- .–	Ottawa : the Board, 1959- . –
7.	Extent Number of volumes. –	vol. –	vol. –
9.	Notes Additional information. –		Also available in French. –
10.	Standard number ISSN	ISSN 0821-4202	ISSN 0384-2347

Writers Guild of Alberta. – Newsletter. – Vol. 1, no. 1 (Dec. 1980)-   . –
Edmonton : the Guild, 1980-   . –   vol. – ISSN 0821-4202

National Energy Board. – Annual report. – (1959)-   . – Ottawa : the Board,
1959-   . –   vol. – Also available in French. – ISSN 0384-2347

Author

Entries for serials rarely contain an author field, as the author is generally a corporate body that does not qualify as an author in a bibliography (see Rule 27). An author field is normally included only if the serial is an annual report.

Title

As a rule, the title of the serial publication is recorded as it appears on the title page, the cover or, when there is no cover, the serial's first page. However, it should be verified that the title appearing on the cover or first page is accurate. The layout design on the serial cover or first page does not always present the actual title of the serial. Moreover, the layout design may change. For instance, the title may contain an ampersand ("&")

on one issue and the word "and" on the next, or the use of upper- and lower-case lettering may vary from issue to issue. For these reasons, the title should be verified against other parts of the serial, including the title page, table of contents page, publication information and the copyright information. When there is a discrepancy, the title should be recorded as it appears in the copyright information (or the publication information when no copyright information is given).

Generic Terms

A title that employs a term such as "newsletter", "bulletin" or "journal" to describe a serial published by a corporate body is recorded as it appears on the serial. When the title is not presented consistently (e.g., the cover shows the generic term before the corporate name, and the copyright information gives the generic term after the name) the version recorded in the entry is that given in the copyright or publication information.

> Quarterly review of film studies
> Journal of legal education
> Review of the National Research Council

When the main source of information for the bibliographic entry does not include the corporate name, that name is entered in the secondary author field.

> Bulletin. – Government Travel Management Centre

In the example above, the name of the sponsoring body appears below the title on the cover, but is not part of the title proper. The corporate name is therefore separated from the title in the entry and recorded in the secondary author field.

A cross-reference is given for a serial title that includes a generic term.

> National Research Council. – Review
> **See**
> Review of the National Research Council

For a discussion of the capitalization of serial titles, see Rule 139.

Subtitle

Very few serials have formal subtitles (i.e., a descriptive phrase following the main title and intended as an integral part of the complete title). However, above or below the serial title on the cover or front page, a serial is likely to carry a descriptive phrase, which is intended to clarify and specify the content and focus of the serial for potential buyers. In such a case, the descriptive phrase is part of the serial's overall visual appeal

Cover	Copyright publication information
Maclean's	MACLEAN's
Canada's weekly	
newsmagazine	
Probe post	Probe post
Canada's environmental	
magazine	
Country estate	Country estate
The country lifestyle	
magazine	
CCM	CIPS computer magazine for
CIPS COMPUTER	computer professionals
MAGAZINE	
for computer professionals	

rather than a formal subtitle. When a descriptive phrase appears consistently with the main title on the serial, it is considered to be a subtitle.

When the descriptive phrase is considered to be a subtitle, it is recorded in the entry immediately after the title.

> Antiques and art : the magazine for fine art collectors and investors

Secondary Author

The "secondary author" of a serial publication is the corporate body (not the commercial publisher) under whose auspices the serial is published. This sponsoring body is listed in the entry to distinguish its function from that of the commercial publisher. It is also used as a means of distinguishing a serial with a generic title from other serials with the same generic title. Sponsoring bodies are most commonly connected with serial publications issued by associations, universities and government departments. The name of the sponsoring body is usually found in the publication information or copyright information.

> Middle East focus. – Canadian Academic Foundation for
> Peace in the Middle East

Edition

When a serial is published in more than one version, the content of each version being different in part or in whole from the content of every other version, each version constitutes a different edition.

The edition may vary according to geographic location, linguistic community, or the kind of textual difference that exists among the editions of the serial.

Canadian ed.

Abridged ed.

Edition information about the serial is usually found in the publication information or copyright information and may also appear on the serial's cover, title page, first page or table of contents page.

Issue Designation

The issue designation lists the volume(s), the number(s) and date(s) of the serial run that is relevant to the bibliography.

Whenever possible, information regarding the issue designation should be obtained from the serial itself. Occasionally, the serial's publication information contains general information (e.g., "MACLEAN'S, established in 1905, is published and printed weekly ..."). The first year of the serial's publication may also be inferred from the specific numerical description or date of a particular issue (e.g., the description "Vol. 80, no. 4" implies that the serial has been published for eighty years. However, because a serial may change publication frequency (e.g., change from a monthly to a weekly), temporarily suspend publication, or change its numbering system, the individual issue description alone is not reliable evidence for the serial's first date of publication. For these reasons, information should be obtained from the relevant physical issues of the serial run cited in the entry.

When it is impossible to examine the physical issues, the issue designation should be verified in reference sources. Useful sources include:

Ulrich's international periodicals directory

Irregular serials and annuals

The IMS Ayer directory of publications

The standard periodical directory

New serial titles : a union list of serials held by libraries in the United States and Canada

Canadian serials directory = Répertoire des publications sériées canadiennes

The union list of serials in libraries of the United States and Canada

Union list of serials in the social sciences and humanities held by Canadian libraries = Liste collective des publications en série dans le domaine des sciences sociales et humaines, dans les bibliothèques canadiennes

Union list of scientific serials in Canadian libraries = Catalogue collectif des publications scientifiques dans les bibliothèques canadiennes

Union list of Canadian newspapers held by Canadian libraries = Liste collective des journaux canadiens disponibles dans les bibliothèques canadiennes

and appropriate automated data bases.

The conventions for the issue designation field are given in Rules 86-90 of Part One.

Publication Data

As with books, publication data about serials includes the following: place of publication, publisher's name, and the year in which the first issue of the serial relevant to the bibliography was published.

Change of Place of Publication or Publisher

If there was a change in the place of publication or the publisher, the publication data field lists the place and publisher relevant to the serial run cited in the entry.

When the serial run recorded in the bibliographic entry includes issues published in more than one place or by more than one publisher, the place or publisher relevant to the first serial issue entered is recorded in the publication data field, and information on any other place or publisher is given in a note.

> Abstracts of English Studies. – Vol 1, no. 1 (Jan 1958)-   . – Boulder : National Council of Teachers of English, 1958-   . – Volumes 24 and subsequent volumes published by the Editorial Board, English Department, University of Calgary, Calgary, Alberta

Date of Publication

The bibliographic entry records the year in which the first issue of the serial relevant to the bibliography was published. The year is followed by a hyphen, four spaces and a period. If the serial has ceased publication or if a limited number of issues are cited in the entry, the hyphen is followed by the year in which the final issue was published, and a period.

> Canadian heritage. – Vol 10, no. 5 (Dec 1984/Jan 1985)-   . – Toronto : Heritage Canada Foundation, 1985-
>
> Quest. – Vol. 1, no. 1 (May 1972)-Vol. 13, no. 8 (Dec. 1984). – Toronto : Comac Communications, 1972-1984

Extent

The extent field lists the number of volumes comprised by the serial run. This number is expressed in Arabic numerals and followed by the abbreviation for "volume" in lower case (e.g., 12 vol.). For a serial that is still being published, the number is replaced by four spaces.

Notes

The purposes of notes include the following:

- to communicate information given on the serial cover, first page or table of contents page.

    Additional statement on cover : For kids 10 to 15

- to outline the publishing and bibliographic history of the serial, such as title changes.

    Continues: *VSO, Vancouver Symphony Orchestra*

- to describe the frequency of the serial.

    Monthly

    Appears three times per year

See Rule 123 for the main purposes of notes.

4. *Examples*

Change of serial title

If a serial that has undergone one or more title changes must be recorded in the bibliography under more than one of the titles, a separate entry is created for each relevant title. Each entry includes cross-references to the other titles of the serial.

Maritime art. – Vol. 1, no. 1 (October 1940)-vol. 3, no. 5 (July 1943). – Halifax : Maritime Art Association, 1940-1943. – 3 vol. – Followed by Canadian art

Canadian art. – Vol. 1, no. 1 (October-November 1943)-vol. 23, no. 4 (October 1966). – Toronto : Society for Art Publications, 1943-1966. – 23 vol. – Follows Maritime art. – Followed by artscanada

Change of Serial Title with No Change of Numbering

The new title is entered, followed by the numbering at which it begins.

Canadian Library Council bulletin. – Vol. 1, no. 1 (October 1944)-vol. 2, no. 5 (June 1946). – Ottawa : Canadian Library Council, 1944-1946. – 2 vol. – Followed by Canadian Library Association bulletin

Canadian Library Association bulletin. – Vol. 3, no. 1 (October 1946)-vol. 16, no. 5 (March 1960). – Ottawa : Canadian Library Association, 1946-1960. – 14 vol. – Formerly Canadian Library Council bulletin. – Followed by Canadian Library

Canadian library. – Canadian Library Association. – Vol. 16, no. 6 (May 1960)-vol. 26, no. 6 (November-December 1969). – Ottawa : Canadian Library Association, 1960-1969. – 10 vol. – Formerly Canadian Library Association bulletin. – Followed by Canadian Library Journal

Canadian library journal. – Canadian Library Association. Vol. 27, no. 1 (January-February 1970)-   . – Ottawa : Canadian Library Association, 1970-
–   vol. – Formerly Canadian library. – ISSN 0008-4352

Serial that has Ceased Publication

artscanada. – Vol. 24, no. 1 (January 1967)-vol. 39, no. 1 (November 1982). – Toronto : Society for Art Publications, 1967-1982. – 15 vol. – Formerly Canadian art

Merger of Two Serial Publications

When a serial incorporates or takes over another serial, the merger is recorded in a note. Cross-references are provided for each title.

The Canadian author and bookman. – Vol. 17, no. 1 (April 1940)-   . – Toronto : Canadian Authors' Association, 1940-   . – vol. – Unites The Canadian author and The Canadian bookman. – ISSN 0008-2937

The Canadian author   **SEE** The Canadian author and bookman

The Canadian bookman **SEE** The Canadian author and bookman

Serials with the Same Title

If the serial recorded could be confused with another serial that bears the same title, the entry should provide appropriate identifying details — usually the place of publication, enclosed in parentheses after the serial title. The publisher's name should also be included if the two serials are published in the same place.

Canadian review (Orlando, Fla.). – Vol. 1, no. 1 (October 1983)-   . – Orlando : University of Central Florida, Canadian Studies Centre, 1983-   . –   vol.

Canadian review (Ottawa). – Vol. 1, no. 1 (February 1974)-vol. 4, no. 4 (June, 1977). – Ottawa : Cooper House Magazine, 1974-1977. – 4 vol. – ISSN 03151190

Serial Subsection

When a serial subsection has been designated by a letter or number, rather than by an independent title, the bibliographic entry records the title of the parent serial and includes enough information to identify the subsection.

Canadian Journal of Research. Section F

Newspapers

An issue of a newspaper may have an individual number, but newspapers are seldom published in volumes. Moreover, newspapers often change ownership, title, publishing schedule and frequency. For these reasons, the first year of publication under the current title generally is used as an issue designation in an entry for a complete newspaper run. However, when the issue designation information present on the newspaper includes a description of volumes or numbers, and the information is prominently displayed and may be useful to the bibliography's users, it can be included in the issue designation field.

> Inuksuk. – Vol. 7, no. 7 (Feb. 9, 1973)-vol. 4, no. 22 (June 30, 1976). – Iqaluit (Frobisher Bay), N.W.T.: [s.n.], 1973-1976. – 4 Vol. – Text in English and Inuktitut. – Continued by: Nunatsiaq news. – ISSN 0702-7923

> Nunatsiaq news. – Vol. 4, no. 23 (July 7, 1976). – Iqaluit, N.W.T. : [s.n.], 1976-   . – vol. – Continues: Tnuksuk. - ISSN 0702-7915

5. Entry for a Single Serial Issue

A bibliographic entry for only one issue of a serial run contains the same elements as are found in an entry for an entire serial run, with the following modifications:
- The issue designation field contains only the numbering of the single serial issue.
- The publication date is the year in which the single serial issue was published.
- The extent field is omitted.
- The notes field contains information relevant to the particular serial issue entered.

6. Examples

Periodical

> Quill & quire. – Vol. 51, no. 4 (April 1985). – Toronto : Key Publishers, 1985. – 50th anniversary issue. – ISSN 0033-6491

Annual Report

> Canada. Information Commissioner. – Annual report. – (1987/88). – Ottawa : the Commissioner, c1988. – ISSN 0826-9904

Directory

> Department of Regional Industrial Expansion. Construction and Capital Markets Directorate. – Directory of Canadian architects. – (1988). – Ottawa : the Department, 1988. – ISSN 0842-6708

Bilingual Directory

> Association of Translators and Interpreters of Ontario. – Répertoire = Directory. – (1986). – Ottawa : the Association, 1986. – ISSN 0226-8868

7. Entry for a Serial Part

In most bibliographies, entries for serial parts are more common than entries for serial runs. Among other things, a serial part may be an essay, story, poem, column, or letter, or a special feature peculiar to a specific serial title.

Illustration no. 21 shows the fields and elements required in an entry for a serial part, as opposed to an entire serial run or a single serial issue. The field numbers are those described in the general entry outline for a document part, in Rule 4.

8. Special Bibliographic Features

The subtitle of the part is recorded exactly as it appears at the head of the part. It should not be taken from the table of contents, which may list an abbreviated or modified form of the subtitle.

Description in the Table of Contents	Title at the Head of the Part
Home hardware : saving time, money and sanity in the studio	Home hardware : saving time (and $anity) in the studio

A direct and reliable point of access in a data base, the ISSN is an indispensable element for document identification, particularly as many serials have the same title (e.g., Forum, News, Bulletin).

The location of the part in the serial (i.e., the pages where the part appears) is indicated by the abbreviation for "page" ("P", capitalized because it opens the field), followed by the numbers of the first and last pages, in Arabic numerals. Consecutive page numbers are separated by a hyphen without spaces (e.g., P. 17-32), and discontinuous page numbers are separated by a comma and space (e.g., P. 20, 66).

9. Examples

Article in a Periodical

McDonald, Dawn. – «Windsor : could you live there?» – Chatelaine. – Vol. 46, no. 2 (February 1976). – ISSN 00000000. – P. 34-36, 50-53

Interview

Ewen, Paterson. – «Paterson Ewen : rain». – Interview with Nick Johnson. – artscanada. – Vol. 38, nos. 2/3, issue 244/245 and 246/247 (March 1982). – Originally published in artscanada, vol. 32, no. 1, issue 196/197, March 1975. – ISSN 0004-4113. – P. 131-132

Newspaper Article

King, Charles. «The NDP acquires a senior citizen». – The Ottawa citizen. – Vol. 130, no. 297 (June 20, 1973). – P. 6

«Sad little shoplifter ends up playing a happier tune». – Whitehorse star. – Vol. 89, no. 75 (April 18, 1989). – P. 18

ENTRY OUTLINE FOR SERIAL PARTS   Illustration no. 21

No. FIELD	ELEMENTS
Part	
1. Author of the part Personal or corporate name. –	Potter, Janice. –
2. Title of the part «Title alternative title, subtitle : parallel title». –	«Patriarchy and paternalism : the case of the Eastern Ontario Loyalist women». –
Host document	
2. Serial title Title alternative title : subtitle = parallel title. –	Ontario history. –
3. Secondary author Name of the sponsoring body. –	Ontario Historical Society. –
5. Issue designation Volume, number (date). –	Vol. 81, no. 1(March 1989). –
9. Notes Additional information. –	
10. Standard number ISSN.–	ISSN 0030-2953. –
11. Location in host document	P. 3-24

Part of a Bilingual Serial

(See also Chapter 6, "Bilingual Documents".)

Laurier, Andrée. – «Gerry Boulet lives to tell the story in his new album». – The Canadian composer = Le compositeur canadien. – Composers, Authors and Publishers Association of Canada. – No. 237 (January 1989). Also appears in French: «Rendez-vous avec Gerry». – P. 8-10

Potter, Janice. – «Patriarchy and paternalism : the case of the Eastern Ontario Loyalist women». – Ontario history. – Ontario Historical Society. – Vol. 81, no. 1 (March 1989). – ISSN 00302953. – P. 3-24

Part Published in Several Issues

When the part is published in several issues, each part is listed in a separate entry.

Hudson, Andrew. «On the critics : the state of responsive awareness». – Canadian art. – Vol. 23, no. 2 (whole no. 101, April 1966). – P. 23-24

Hudson, Andrew. «On the critics : 2 : the critic and the artist». – Canadian art. – Vol. 23, no. 3 (whole no. 102, July 1966). – P. 34-35

Section 12
Slides and Filmstrips

An entry for a set of slides or a filmstrip should contain the fields and elements shown in Illustration no. 22. The field numbers are those described in the general entry outline in Rule 3.

1. Scope

This section establishes the conventions for bibliographic entries for slides and filmstrips. These document types are discussed together because they have common features. Both are produced on the same physical medium, 16- or 35-mm film, but the slides are cut, whereas the filmstrip is not. A sample entry for one slide is presented in Part 6 of this section.

2. *Bibliographic Information Source*

The information required to create a bibliographic entry for a set of slides or a filmstrip is usually found on the first or last frames of the work. Some information may also appear on the wrapper or container or on the documentation accompanying the work. If these sources do not list all the bibliographic information, it should be obtained from reference works and enclosed in brackets, in accordance with Rule 11.

3. *Special Bibliographic Features*

An entry for a set of slides or a filmstrip is usually listed under the title. The title field should contain a descriptive identifier — e.g., "slide set" or "filmstrip" — expressed in lower case and in the singular, and enclosed in brackets, immediately after the title or alternative title, in accordance with Rule 64.

The secondary author field contains the name(s) and role description(s) of individuals who participated in the production of the work in some capacity (e.g., a producer or graphic artist) and the name of the corporate body that commissioned the document.

The extent field lists the number of physical units that make up the work, followed by the document descriptor (e.g., 42 slides, 2 filmstrips).

ENTRY OUTLINE FOR SLIDES AND FILMSTRIPS *Illustration no. 22*

No. FIELD	ELEMENTS	
	Slides	**Filmstrips**
2. Title Title alternative title [descriptive identifier] : subtitle = parallel title. –	The western civilization slide collection [slide set]. –	All about bicycles - and libraries, too! [filmstrip] . –
3. Secondary author Name of producer, graphic artist, organization that commissioned the document. –		National Library of Canada and National Film Board of Canada. –
6. Publication data Place : production company, date. –	Annapolis, Md. : Instructional Resources Corporation, c1982. –	[S.I.] : National Film Board of Canada, 1984. –
7. Extent number of physical units. –	2 100 slides. –	1 filmstrip. –
8. Series (Title ; numbering). –		
9. Notes Additional information	Col. – Includes guide to the collection, 253 p., ed. Judy A. Reardon and Raymond W. Smock	Col. – Includes 1 audio cassette

Slides

The western civilization slide collection [slide set]. – Annapolis, Md. :
Instructional Resources Corporation, c1982. – 2 100 slides. – Col. – Includes
guide to the collection, 253 p., ed. Judy A. Reardon and Raymond W. Smock

Filmstrip

All about bicycles - and libraries, too! [filmstrip] – Directed by Jocelyn Rehder,
presented by the National Library of Canada. – [S.I.] : National Film Board of
Canada, 1984. – 1 filmstrip. – Col. – Includes 1 audio cassette

The notes field provides the following information:
* the document title if the document is available in another language and the title
  may be easily ascertained
* the distributor's name and address if the document is not easily accessible
* the abbreviation "col." or "b&w" to indicate whether the document is in colour
  or in black and white
* the presence of any accompanying document (e.g., a cassette, pamphlet or
  poster)
* whether the document is available in other forms.

4. Examples

Accompanying Documents

Safety [filmstrip] : a way of life. – Toronto : Moreland-Latchford Productions, c1974. – 4 filmstrips. – Col. – Titles : «Traffic safety», «Home safety», «Transit safety», «School safety». – Each filmstrip accompanied by an audiocassette

Distributor's Name

Human geography of Canada [filmstrip]. – Toronto : International Cinemedia Center, c1978. – 8 filmstrips. – Distributed by Visual Education Centre, 75 Horner Ave., Unit 1, Toronto, Ontario M8Z 4X5. – Each filmstrip accompanied by an audiocassette

5. Entry for One Slide

An entry for a single slide should list the following information, in accordance with the entry outline for a document part (see Rule 4):
- the slide title, enclosed in angle quotes, in accordance with Rule 68 and
- the required information about the host document (i.e., the set of slides).

6. Example

«Snowshoes hanging on cabin». – The beatitude people [slide set]. – Produced by Margaret Denis. – Ottawa : Canadian Catholic Conference, 1973. – 200 slides. – Col. – Slide no. 66

Section 13
Sound Recordings

An entry for a sound recording contains the fields and elements shown in Illustration no. 23. The field numbers are those described in the general entry outline in Rule 3.

1. Scope

This section establishes the conventions for entries for records and cassettes.

2. Bibliographic Information Source

The bibliographic information used in entries for sound recordings is taken from the recording label or from the recording wrapper or container (e.g., the record sleeve or cassette box). Bibliographic information may also appear on documentation accompanying the recording. If these sources do not list all the required information, it may be obtained from reference works, in which case it should be enclosed in brackets, in accordance with Rule 11.

3. Special Bibliographic Features

The type of sound recording (record or cassette) is a secondary consideration in the creation of the bibliographic entry. In fact, the nature of the recording's contents determines the elements to be entered, particularly in the author and secondary author fields. For instance, if the recording is a collection of poems by different poets under a general title, the author field will be different from that for a selection of musical pieces by one composer. The various types of recording content and the corresponding elements that should appear in the author or secondary author field are listed below. The rule numbers refer to the rules in Part One of the manual.

The title field contains the descriptive identifier "sound recording", regardless of the type of recording. It is expressed in lower case and in the singular, and enclosed in brackets immediately after the title or alternative title, in accordance with Rule 64 ("Descriptive Identifier").

No. FIELD	ELEMENTS
1. Author Name of composer, author or performer. –	Bach, Johann Sebastian. –
2. Title Title alternative title [descriptive identifier] : subtitle = parallel title. –	Cantatas no. 4 & 140 [sound recording] = Cantates n°s 4 & 140. –
3. Secondary authors Name of songwriter, reader or performer. –	CBC Vancouver Orchestra. –
6. Publication data Label name, date. –	CBC Enterprises, p1984. –
7. Extent Number of physical units. –	1 cassette. –
8. Series (Title ; numbering). –	
9. Notes Additional information	Also available on disc. – Edition no. CBC Enterprises SMC 5029C

Bach, Johann Sebastian. – Cantatas no. 4 & 140 [sound recording] = Cantates no 4 & 140. – CBC Vancouver Orchestra. – CBC Enterprises, p1984. – 1 cassette. – Also available on disc. – Edition no. CBC Enterprises SMC 5029C

The secondary author field lists the names and describes the roles of songwriters, performers (if not already cited in the author field), and readers.

The publication data field contains the name of the production company and the date of manufacture. (Place of publication is never mentioned.) The name of the production company to be preferred and inscribed in the publication data field is the name that appears predominantly on the recording label. The date of manufacture is usually identified in the production information by the initial "p" within a circle. Note that any copyright date appearing on the recording refers to the publication date of the recorded work(s) and not the date of the recording. Other dates (e.g., the design date for a record sleeve or an accompanying document) may also sometimes appear on the recording or its wrapper. These dates should not be confused with each other.

The extent field lists the number of physical units, followed by a document descriptor (e.g., 2 cassettes, 1 digital sound recording) and the playing speed of tape reels and analog disc recordings.

SPECIAL BIBLIOGRAPHIC FEATURES

Content of recording	Rule	ELEMENTS	
		Author field	Secondary Author Field
Texts by one author	15	Writer	Narrator
Texts by several authors under general title	50	Title (individual texts and their authors may be cited in a note)	Narrator, compiler if any
Texts by several authors with no general title	53	First author's name followed by title of individual work, second author's name followed by title of individual work, and third author's name followed by title of individual work	Narrator
Musical works by one composer	15	Composer	Performer (artist, group, orchestra)
Musical works with lyrics	43	Composer	Songwriter, performer (artist, group orchestra)
Musical pieces by several composers under general title	52	Performer (individual works and their authors may be listed in a note)	
Musical pieces by several composers with no general title	55	First composer's name followed by title of individual work, second composer's name followed by title of individual work, and third composer's name followed by title of individual work	Performer (artist, group, orchestra)
Classical music	55	Performer	
Popular music	56		

The notes field may provide the following information:

- the name of any person associated with the sound recording if that name is not listed in the author or secondary author fields but is important to the bibliography (e.g., the cast of a play or an opera)
- the presence of any accompanying documents (e.g., printed lyrics or a poster)
- whether the sound recording is available in other forms
a list of the works included under a general title
- the publisher's number (i.e., the commercial reference or catalogue number); this number is preceded by the commercial name of the publisher, as given on the label.

4. Examples

Work by a Writer

Mowat, Farley. – Never cry wolf [sound recording]. – Read by Ryan Halloran. – Toronto : Canadian National Institute for the Blind, c1975. – 4 cassettes

Works by a Composer

Ravel, Maurice. – Louis Lortie joue Maurice Ravel [sound recording] = Louis Lortie plays Maurice Ravel. – CBC Enterprises, p1985. – 1 disc, 33 1/3 r/min. – Contains: Gaspard de la nuit, Sonatine, La valse. – Edition no., Musica Viva MV1010

Offenbach, Jacques. – Les contes d'Hoffman [sound recording] = The tales of Hoffman. – Orchestre de la Suisse romande. – Decca, 1986. – 2 analog discs. – Soloists: Placido Domingo, Joan Sutherland, Gabriel Bacquier. – Edition no. Decca 417363-2 DH2

Finaldi, Angelo. – Dioxine de carbone et son rayon rose [sound recording] : un opéra cartoon. – Luc Plamondon, paroles, Diane Dufresne, interprète. – Kébec-disk, p1984. – 1 disc, 33 1/3 r/min. – With booklet. – Also available on cassette. – Edition no. Kébec-Disk KD-607

Works by Several Composers under General Title

Toronto Mendelssohn Choir. – Gloria [sound recording]. – Elmer Iseler, conductor. – RCA Victor, p1968. – 1 disc, 33 1/3 r/min. – Contains: «Jubilate deo» by Gabrieli; «Ave maria» by Rachmaninoff; «On this day earth shall ring» by H.C. Stewart; «Coelos ascendit hodie» by Charles Villiers Stanford; «Come, thou beloved of Christ» by Healey Willan; «Children's Christmas song» and «God bless the master» from Folk songs of the four seasons by Vaughn Williams; «An apostrophe to the heavenly hosts» by Healey Willan; «Gloria» by Harry Somers. – Edition no. RCA Victor LSC-3054. – Includes pamphlet with lyrics

Dufresne, Diane. – Follement votre [sound recording]. – Amérilys, p1986. – 1 disc, 33 1/3 r/min. – Contains: Parlez-moi d'amour, Les dessous chics, La vie en rose, Ich bin von kopf bis fuss auf liebe eingestellt, Fascination, Somewhere over the rainbow, Ils s'aiment, Addio del passato, J'tombe amoureuse. – Also available on cassette. – Edition no. Amérilys AM 1001

Hachey, Bobby. – Mon sourire . . . [sound recording]. – Bonanza, [s.d.]. – 1 cassette. – Contains: Mon sourire, ma limousine; Tu es là dans mes pensées; Pour t'oublier; Pretty woman; Celle qui sert aux tables; Cela est impossible; Quand papa tenait maman; Fraulein; Dis-moi combien de temps; Ma belle au bois dormant. – Edition no. Bonanza 519-29737

Works by Several Composers with No General Title

Franck, César. – Symphony in d minor [sound recording] = Symphonie en ré mineur = Symphony in D-moll. – Berlioz, Hector. – King Lear = Le Roi Lear = Konig Lear. – Vancouver Symphony Orchestra, Kazuyoshi Akiyama, conductor. – CBC Enterprises, p1985. – 1 disc, 33 1/3 r/min. – Also available on cassette. – Edition no. CBC SM 5033

Section 14
Works of Art

A bibliographic entry for a work of art contains the fields and elements shown in Illustration no. 25. The field numbers are those described in the general entry outline in Rule 3.

1. Scope

This section establishes the conventions for entries for graphic works and three-dimensional objects, whether unique, published or replicated, or reproduced.

Graphic works are artistic representations produced on a flat surface (e.g., paper, canvas or wood) by one or more techniques (e.g., drawing, painting, etching or printing). The technique may involve one or more types of material (e.g., a drawing may be done in ink, pencil or both; a painting may be done in oils or watercolours).

Three-dimensional objects include sculptures and installation art.

2. Bibliographic Information Source

Bibliographic information for works of art is taken from the work itself, from an information source provided by the owner of the work or from other reference sources. Information taken from sources other than the work itself should be enclosed in brackets, in accordance with Rule 11.

3. Special Bibliographic Features

If the bibliography cites two or more works by the same artist, but the signature appears in a different style on some of the works, one form of the signature should be selected and used consistently throughout the bibliography (see Rule 20).

The publication data field contains only the date of the work's creation.

The extent field gives the dimensions of the work — the height and width of graphic works, and only the height of three-dimensional objects. The frame or mounting size are not included in the dimensions of a graphic work.

ENTRY OUTLINE FOR WORKS OF ART

No. FIELD	ELEMENTS	
	Graphic work	**Work in three dimensions**
1. Author Artist's name. –	Jordaens, Jacob. –	Puget, Pierre. –
2. Title Title alternative title : subtitle = parallel title. –	As the old sing, so the young pipe. –	Bust of a king. –
6. Publication data Only the date of creation. –	[1640?]. –	[1670?]. –
7. Extent Dimensions. –	145.5 x 218 cm. –	71.1 cm. –
9. Notes Additional information. –	Oil on canvas. – National Gallery of Canada, Ottawa	Carrara marble with slightly brownish patina. – National Gallery of Canada, Ottawa

Graphic Work

Jordaens, Jacob. – As the old sing, so the young pipe. – [1640?]. – 145.5 x 218 cm. – Oil on canvas. – National Gallery of Canada, Ottawa

Work in Three Dimensions

Puget, Pierre. – Bust of a king. – [1670?]. – 71.1 cm. – Carrara marble with slightly brownish patina. – National Gallery of Canada, Ottawa

The notes field may provide the following information:
- a description of the various styles of signature used by the artist
- the technique (e.g., drawing, painting or etching), the material(s) (e.g., ink, watercolours or marble) and the medium (e.g., paper, canvas or wood)
- the identification number if there are several originals of the work (e.g., 2/15)
- the repository of the work

4. Examples

Unique Works

A Graphic Work

Jackson, A.Y. – The red maple. – 1914. – 79 x 97 cm. – Oil on canvas. – National Gallery of Canada, Ottawa

A Three-Dimensional Object

> Moore, Henry. – Three way piece-points. – 1964. – 64 cm. – Bronze. – National Library of Canada, Ottawa. – Presented to Canada by Britain in 1967 in celebration of the Centenary of Confederation

Published or replicated works (several originals)

There may be several examples, all originals, of a work of art, as is the case when a limited edition of a print has been issued, each print showing the same pictorial representation but bearing a unique number within the edition. Another such instance occurs when several statues have been cast from the same mould.

> Riopelle, Jean-Paul. – Cap Tourmente. – [1983?]. – 94 cm. – 13 lithographs in a portfolio. – 28/60. – Rare Book Collection, National Library of Canada, Ottawa

Reproductions

In an entry for a reproduction of a work of art (i.e., not the original work itself), the following information should be recorded: the artist's name, the title of the reproduced work, in quotation marks as specified in Rule 68 and details about the reproduction's location (e.g., book, periodical, set of slides, or microfiche). Any available information about the original work is given in a note.

Reproduction in a Book

> Renoir, Auguste. – «Le petit paysage». – The graphic work of Renoir : catalogue raisonné. – Compiled by Dr. Joseph G. Stella. – [S.l. : s.n., s.d.]. – Etching; 7.9 x 15.5 cm; [1908?]; Art Institute of Chicago. – Plate 21

Reproduction in a Periodical

> Bruskin, Grisha. – «Alefbet». – Art in America. – Vol. 77, no. 4 (April 1989). – Oil on canvas; 127 x 105 cm; 1985; Struve Gallery, Chicago. – ISSN 0004-3214. – P. 65

Reproduction on a Slide

> Jackson, A.Y. – «Gatineau River» [slide]. – [Toronto] : Art Gallery of Ontario, [s.d.]. – Col. – Oil on panel; 26.7 x 34.2 cm; 1963; Ontario Heritage Foundation, Firestone Art Collection. – Slide no. AR70

CHAPTER 5
Special Types of Documents

Section 1
Conference Proceedings

1. Scope

Conference proceedings are the collected presentations given at a conference, seminar, workshop, meeting or other gathering of individuals or representatives of corporate bodies.

2. Recording Rules

A bibliographic entry for the proceedings of a conference follows the conventions for the document format in question. For instance, if the conference proceedings are published in book form, the entry is created in accordance with the conventions for books; and if the document is available on audio cassette, the entry follows the bibliographic conventions for sound recordings.

3. Special Features

Proceedings as a Whole

When creating an entry for the proceedings of a conference the major difficulty consists of correctly establishing the corporate author.

Since a conference is considered to be a corporate author whose proceedings reflect the collective thought or activity of the conference (see Rules 26 and 27), the name of the conference is recorded in the author field.

When the conference **is not unique** (e.g., when it is one in a number of annual conferences), the numerical designation of the conference is recorded (in ordinal form) after the name of the conference. It should be enclosed in parentheses, along with the year and the location of the conference, with commas separating these bibliographic elements (see Rule 36).

> National Rail Passenger Conference (1st, 1976, Regina)

When the conference **is a "once only" event,** the numerical designation is not given.

Conference on Social Development in a Pluralist Society

If the conference constitutes a **regular activity of an association or organization** and has a non-distinctive or generic name (e.g., annual conference), the bibliography should list the conference proceedings under the corporate name, followed by the term that most accurately describes the event (e.g., "symposium", "colloquium", "conference"), the numerical designation, and the year and location of the event.

Environmental Councils of Canada. Assembly (8th, 1983, Hull)

The title of the conference is entered in the title field. The description "Proceedings of . . ." is included as a subtitle when the title page or other main bibliographic information source indicates that it should be considered as a subtitle. The title page or other main bibliographic information source may give the description "Proceedings of . . ." as the title of the work, in which case it is so recorded in the entry.

The name of the editor or compiler of the proceedings is recorded in the secondary author field.

A note may include information on the agency or agencies that sponsored the conference or on the contents of the work.

Parts of Proceedings

An entry for a part of conference proceedings is similar to an entry for a document part. The entry includes information about the part (i.e., the author and title of the part) and about the host document, in accordance with the conventions for the document format in question.

4. Examples

Proceedings as a Whole

Conference That Is a Regular Event

University of Windsor Seminar on Canadian-American Relations (14th, 1972, Windsor). – Information processing and the right to privacy : a crossroads decision for North Americans : proceedings of the 14th annual University of Windsor seminar on Canadian-American relations, held at the University of Windsor, Windsor, Ontario, 1972. – Edited by J. Alex Murray. – Windsor : University of Windsor Press, 1973. – 139 p.

"Once Only" Conference

Conference on Social Development in a Pluralist Society. – Social development in a pluralist society : proceedings. – Ottawa : Canadian Council on Social Development, c1978. – 189 p. – Also published in French, Le développement social dans une société pluraliste. – ISBN 0-88810-284-4

Conference That Is a Regular Activity of an Association

Environmental Councils of Canada. Assembly (8th, 1983, Hull). – The public role in setting and enforcing environmental standards : role of environmental councils. – [Ottawa] : Supply and Services Canada, c1985. – 61 p. – (CEAC report ; 13). – Organized by Canadian Environmental Advisory Council, Environment Canada. – French title: Le rôle du public dans l'établissement et l'application des normes environnementales : rôle des Conseils de l'environnement. – ISBN 0-662-139771-1

Part of Proceedings

In a Book

Campbell, Robert, R. – «A student's point of view». – Workshop on the study of athletic programs in Canadian universities (1974, Ottawa). – Proceedings of the Workshop on the study of athletic programs in Canadian universities, Ottawa, November 6, 1974. – Ottawa: Association of Universities and Colleges of Canada, 1974. – P. 25-32

Section 2
Government Documents

1. Scope

This section provides guidelines for the bibliographic description of government documents, which include all materials issued by a body, agency or organization belonging to any level of government. These publications may be legislative texts, policy statements, background papers or annual reports.

2. Recording Rules

An entry for a government document follows the bibliographic conventions for the document format in question. For instance, if the government document is published in book form, the entry is created in accordance with the conventions for books and pamphlets; if the document is published as a microform, the entry follows the conventions for microforms.

Government documents are often published in two languages, in which case the rules governing bilingual documents are applied (see Chapter 6).

3. Special Features

Author

The government body responsible for the work is regarded as the corporate author when the document falls under the following criteria (see Rule 27): the document must be of an administrative nature (e.g. a guide listing rules to be followed in certain cases), must convey the orientations of the body (e.g. a memoir or a declaration) or must describe the activities of the body (e.g. an annual report). When the work does not fall into one or more of these categories, it is entered under the name of the personal author or under the title.

When the government body is regarded as the author of the document, its name is recorded in the entry as it appears on the document, except for the following three cases:

1) Bodies that are identified by the name of a geographic or political jurisdiction. These bodies include:

   a) legislative bodies (e.g., Canada. Parliament)

   b) courts (e.g., Canada. Supreme Court)

   c) chiefs of government and heads of state (e.g., Canada. Prime Minister)

   d) armed services (e.g., Canada. Canadian Armed Forces)

   e) government departments (e.g., Canada. Department of Communications)

   f) embassies, consulates and high commissions (e.g., Canada. Consulate General (San Francisco, U.S.A.))

   g) delegations to international or intergovernmental bodies (e.g., Canada. Canadian Commission for Unesco)

   h) commissions of inquiry, task forces and other bodies appointed by government to carry out a specific task (e.g., Canada. Commission of Inquiry into Part-Time Work).

2) Government bodies that have generic names (e.g., Ontario. Commission on Employment Relations).

3) Government bodies whose names indicate subordination to a larger government body. In accordance with Rule 29, the name of the subordinate body is preceded by the name of the parent body.

The conventions for capitalizing the names of subordinate government bodies are given in Rule 134.

Secondary Author

When the work is entered under the name of the corporate author or under the title, the name of the personal author (if shown on the work) is recorded in the secondary author field. When the work is produced by a committee, commission or similar body, the name of the chairperson, commissioner or person with similar responsibility is entered in the secondary author field if the work lists the responsibility of that person (e.g., "coordinated by Jean Ducharme"). If the work does not cite the person's role, this information may be given in a note (e.g., "Commissioner was Mr. Donald Macdonald").

Publication Data

The copyright holder for the work is not necessarily the publisher. When the government body that has issued the work is presented as the work's publisher, or appears to be the publisher, that body is listed as such in the entry. When the name of the publisher cannot be determined from the work or other relevant information sources, the government agency responsible for the work is assumed to be the publisher. The name of the distributor or printing agency (e.g., Department of Supply and Services) may be given as the publisher's name in the absence of all other information about the publisher.

4. Examples

Document Recorded under Name of Corporate Author

Canada. Department of National Defence. – Challenge and commitment : a defence policy for Canada. – Ottawa : the Department, c1987. – 89 p. – Also published in French, entitled Défis et engagements. – DSS catalogue no. D2-73/1987E. – ISBN 0-660-12509-9

Canada. Canadian Government Office of Tourism. – Tourism in Canada : past, present, future. – Ottawa : the Office, 1982. – 72 p. – Also published in French, entitled Le tourisme au Canada : le passé, le présent, et l'avenir. – DSS catalogue no. C86-24/1983E. – ISBN 0-662-12407-3

Commission of Inquiry

Canada. Royal Commission of Inquiry into Working Conditions in the Post Office Department. – [Report]. – Commissioner Hon. André Montpetit. – Ottawa : Queen's Printer, 1966. – 363 p. – French title: Commission royale d'enquête sur les conditions de travail au ministère des postes. – Cat. no. Z1-1965-2

Canada. Commission of Inquiry on Unemployment Insurance. – Summary report. – Ottawa : Supply and Services Canada, 1986. – 83 p. – Also available in French, La commission d'enquête sur l'assurance-chômage. – DSS catalogue no. MP15-15/1986-1E. – ISBN 0-660-12214-6

Ontario. Commission on the Future Development of the Universities of Ontario. – Ontario universities : options and futures. – [Toronto] : the Commission, 1984. – 64 p. – Also published in French, entitled Les universités de l'Ontario : options pour l'avenir

Document Recorded under Name of Personal Author

MacNeill, J.W. – Environmental management. – Prepared for the Privy Council Office, Government of Canada. – Ottawa : Information Canada, 1971. – 191 p. – French title, La gestion du milieu. – Cat no. CP32-12/1971

Serial Publication

National Energy Board. – Annual report. – (1959)-   . – Ottawa : the Board, 1959-   . – vol. – Also available in French: Rapport annuel. – ISBN 0-662-15621-1

Environment Canada. – Canada water year book. – (1975). – Ottawa : Information Canada, 1975. – 232 p. – DSS Cat. no. En36425/1975. – Departmental req. no. KL 398-4-2357. – Also available in French: Annuaire de l'eau du Canada

Section 3
Legal Documents

1. Scope

This section deals with legal documents, including statutes, bills, regulations and cases.

2. Recording Rules

An entry for a legal document follows the conventions for the document format in question. For instance, if the document is published in book form, the entry is created in accordance with the bibliographic conventions for books and pamphlets, and an entry for a legal document published as a microform follows the conventions for microforms. For bilingual legal documents, the rules governing bilingual documents are applied (see Chapter 6).

3. Special Features

STATUTES

Entries for statutes or acts are listed under the name of the government, or jurisdiction, that legislated the statute (e.g., Canada, Quebec or New Brunswick). The title field contains the short title of the act, which is given in the first or last section of the document. When the act has no short title, the long title at the head of the text is used. If the year in which the act was passed is of particular importance to the bibliography, it is given in a note.

EXAMPLES

Act Published as Separate Document

Nova Scotia. – Trade union act : Statutes of Nova Scotia, ch. 19, proclaimed October 1, 1972. – Halifax : Queen's Printer, 1972. – vii, 65 p.

Act Published as Separate Bilingual Document

Nova Scotia. – Human rights act : Statutes of Nova Scotia, ch. 11 [amended to 1986]. – Halifax : Queen's Printer, 1986. – 19,22 p. – Text in English and French with French text on inverted pages. – Title of additional t.p.: Loi sur les droits de la personne

Act Published In a Larger Work

Canada. «Postal services interruption relief act = Loi de réparation consécutive à une interruption des services postaux». – Revised statutes of Canada = Statuts révisés du Canada. – Ottawa : Queen's Printer, 1985. – English and French text in parallel columns. – Ch. P-16

Prince Edward Island. – «Lightning rod act». – Revised statutes of Prince Edward Island. – Charlottetown : Queen's Printer, 1974. – Ch. L-16, p. 1633-1638

Volume or Set of Statute Volumes

Prince Edward Island. – Revised statutes of Prince Edward Island. – Charlottetown : Queen's Printer, 1974. – 3 vol.

BILLS

The bibliographic entry for a bill is listed under the bill number followed by the title of the bill. The notes field should contain the following information:
- The parliamentary calendar date, i.e. the number of the legislature and session, as well as the publication year. This information is crucial to accurately identify bills, since their numbering changes with each session.
- The stage reached by the bill in the legislative process (for ex.: first reading) followed by the date as it appears on the document, including not only the year but also the day and month.

Bill C-207 : an act to recognize hockey as a national sport = Projet de loi C-207 : loi reconnaissant le hockey comme sport national. – [Ottawa] : Queen's Printer, [1988]. – [3] p. – 1st reading, December 22, 1988, 34th Parliament, 1st session (1988). – (1988)

REGULATIONS

A bibliographic entry for a regulation resembles an entry for a statute. The title of the act under which the regulation is promulgated can be given in a note.

EXAMPLES

Regulation Published as Separate Document

New Brunswick. – Regulation 79-69 : teacher certification regulation under the Schools act = Règlement 79-69 : certification des enseignants établie en vertu de la Loi scolaire. – [Fredericton] : Queen's Printer for New Brunswick, [1979]

Ontario. – Ontario regulation 71/84 : (regional tribunals) under the Education act = Règlement de l'Ontario 71/84 : (tribunaux régionaux) pris en application de la Loi de l'éducation. – [Toronto] : Ministry of the Attorney General, 1984. – 5 p. – French and English text on facing pages

Regulation Published In a Larger Work

Canada. – «Life saving equipment regulations = Règlement sur l'équipement de sauvetage». – Consolidated regulations of Canada = Codification des règlements du Canada. – Ottawa : Statute Revision Commission, c1978. – English and French text in parallel columns. – Vol. 16, ch. 1436

Regulation Published In a Serial

Saskatchewan. – «Provincial homestead regulations». – The Saskatchewan gazette. – Vol. 40, no. 13 (April 8, 1944). – P. 13-20

CASES

Decisions and salient details of cases are compiled in volumes called reports or reporters. A bibliographic entry for a case is listed under the title of the case. It should contain the bibliographic fields and elements of the general entry outline for a document part, as described in Rule 4.

The title of the case consists of:

- the plaintiff's name,
- followed by the abbreviation "v." (for "versus") in English, or "c." (for "contre") in French,
- and the defendant's name. Usually, abbreviated forms of the names are used when referring to the case (e.g., "Bell Canada v. Lalonde" rather than "Bell Canada Corporation Ltd. v. Paul Lalonde").

The name of the court that rendered the decision is given in a note if it does not appear in the title of the reporter being used for the entry.

EXAMPLES

«Snyder v. Montreal Gazette». – Canada Supreme Court reports = Recueil des arrêts de la Cour suprême du Canada. – Vol. 1 (1988). – ISSN 0045-4230. – P. 494-512

«Fidelity Trust Co. v. Signature Finance Ltd. et al». – Alberta reports. – Vol. 79 (1987). – Judgement of the Alberta Court of Queen's Bench. – ISSN 0703-3109. – P. 348-351

Section 4
Legislative Documents

1. Scope

This section deals with legislative documents, which include documents issued by legislative bodies (e.g., Parliament, National Assembly or Legislative Assembly). The guidelines below apply to Debates, Minutes of Proceedings and Evidence, Journals, Order Papers and Notices, and Gazettes. The federal, provincial, regional and municipal governments of Canada produce some or all of these documents; the titles of the documents may vary from government to government.

2. Recording Rules

Entries for legislative documents follow the bibliographic conventions for serial publications. Legislative documents are, in fact, published over an indefinite period of time in several successive parts, identified by numbers and dates. For bilingual official documents, the rules governing bilingual documents are applied.

3. Special Features

The author field lists:
- the level of government, or jurisdiction (e.g., Canada, Quebec or Ontario),
- the legislative body (e.g., Parliament. Senate; Parliament. House of Commons; National Assembly; Legislative Assembly), and
- when applicable, any other body appointed by the legislative body (e.g., a committee or subcommittee). In accordance with Rule 29, all these names are entered in descending order of importance. The conventions for capitalizing the names of government bodies are given in Rule 133.

The issue designation field contains the dates (in parentheses), preceded by the numbers of the legislature and session.

4. Examples

Debates

Canada. Parliament. House of Commons. – House of Commons debates : official report. – 32nd Parliament, 1st session, vol. 21 (9 March 1983-21 April 1983). – Ottawa : Queen's Printer for Canada, 1983

Canada. Parliament. Senate. – Debates of the Senate of the Dominion of Canada. – 5th Parliament, 3rd session, vol. 2 (28 April 1885-20 July 1885). – Ottawa : Holland Bros., 1885

MacDonald, Flora. – «Communications : closure of CNCP telegraph offices». – Canada. Parliament. House of Commons. – House of Commons debates : official report. – 32nd Parliament, 1st session, vol. 21 (9 March 1983-21 April 1983). – Ottawa : Queen's Printer for Canada, 1983. – P. 23645

Minutes

Canada. Parliament. Senate. Special Committee on Poverty. – Proceedings of the Special Senate Committee on Poverty. – 28th Parliament, 3rd session, no. 11 (November 10, 1970). – Ottawa : Queen's Printer for Canada, 1970

Canada. Parliament. House of Commons. Standing Committee on Justice and Legal Affairs. – Minutes of proceedings and evidence of the Standing Committee on Justice and Legal Affairs = Procès-verbaux et témoignages du Comité permanent de la justice et des questions juridiques. – 30th Parliament, 1st session, no. 3 (19 November 1974). – Ottawa : Queen's Printer for Canada, 1974

Whitney, (Laurel). – [Comments on Canadian aid to refugees]. – Canada. Parliament. House of Commons. Special Committee on the Peace Process in Central America. – Minutes of proceedings and evidence on the Special Committee on the Peace Process in Central America = Procès-verbaux et témoignages du Comité spécial sur le processus de pacification en Amérique centrale. – 33rd Parliament, 2nd session, no. 5 (May 3, 1988). – P. 5:32

Section 5
Patent Documents

1. Scope

Patent documents are official documents issued by an authorized agency granting certain exclusive rights (e.g., making or selling) to an article or process. This section provides guidelines for the bibliographic identification of such documents, particularly inventors' certificates.

2. Recording Rules

An entry for a patent document follows the conventions for the document format in question. For instance, if a patent document is in pamphlet form, the entry is created in accordance with the bibliographic conventions for books and pamphlets.

3. Special Features

The name of the patent proprietor is entered in the author field, the title of the invention in the title field, and the names of other persons or organizations associated with the patent (e.g., the inventors) in the secondary author field.

The publication data field contains only the date (day, month and year) that the document was published.

The international classification number and the document identifier (i.e., country, document type and document number) are given in two separate notes.

4. Example

Dominion Bridge Co. Ltd. (Montreal). – Drilling machine. – George W.P. Evans, inventor. – 18 January 1972. – 17 p. – Canadian patent 890686

Section 6
Standards

1. Scope

This section gives guidelines for creating a bibliographic entry for a standard, that is, a work in which an authorized agency records specific criteria and requirements applicable to products and activities under its jurisdiction.

2. Recording Rules

A bibliographic entry for a standard is created in accordance with the conventions for the document format in question. For instance, if the standard is in pamphlet form, the entry follows the bibliographic conventions for books and pamphlets.

3. Special Features

The name of the corporate body responsible for the standard appears in the author field. If the corporate author is also the publisher, its name is given in abbreviated form in the publication data field (see Rule 99 and Rule 155).

The notes field contains the complete or abbreviated name of the standards organization and the number of the standard.

4. Example

Canadian Gas Association. – Lever operated non-lubricated gas shut-off valves. – Don Mills, Ont. : the Association, 1985. – 14 p. – National Standard of Canada, CAN1-3.16-M85. – Approved by Standards Council of Canada

Section 7
Theses

1. Scope

This section provides guidelines for the bibliographic description of a thesis, that is, a scholarly work created for the purpose of obtaining a graduate or post-graduate degree.

2. Recording Rules

An entry for a thesis is created in accordance with the conventions for the document format in question. For instance, if the thesis is unpublished, the entry follows the bibliographic conventions for manuscripts; and if the thesis is published in book form, the entry follows the conventions for books.

3. Special Features

The notes field in a bibliographic entry for a thesis lists the following information:
* the diploma or degree (in abbreviated form) for which the thesis was written,
* the name of the institution where the thesis was presented,
* the year in which the diploma or degree was conferred.

Standard abbreviations for academic degrees and titles can be found in *Reverse acronyms, initialisms & abbreviations dictionary*, ed. Julie E. Towell and Helen E. Sheppard.* If no official abbreviation for a diploma or degree exists, the terms "doctoral" or "master's" is used, as appropriate.

---

* See Bibliography.

4. Examples

Manuscript

Geller, Gloria. – Role aspirations and life-style orientations of high school women. – 149 p. – M.A. thesis, University of Toronto, 1974

Book

Calderisi, Maria. – Music publishing in the Canadas, 1800-1867. – Ottawa : National Library of Canada, 1981. – 128, 124 p. – Additional title on title-page: L'édition musicale au Canada, 1800-1867. – Research begun in preparation for Music publishing in Canada, 1800-1867, M.M.A. thesis, McGill University, 1976. – DSS Cat. no. SN3-128/1981. – ISBN 0-660-50454-5

Microform

Norman, Joanne S. – The psychomachia in medieval art [microform] : metamorphoses of an allergy. – Ottawa : National Library of Canada, 1980. – 4 microfiches. – (Canadian Theses on Microfiche). – Ph.D. thesis, University of Ottawa, 1979

CHAPTER 6
Bilingual Documents

1. Scope

This chapter provides guidelines for creating bibliographic entries for works written in two languages. As Canadian documents are often published in two languages English and French a separate chapter is devoted to this subject. However, this chapter merely elaborates on the general conventions already established for unilingual works. Note that the guidelines given here also apply to multilingual documents.

2. Recording Rules

In general, an entry for a bilingual document is created according to the conventions for the document type in question. For instance, an entry for a bilingual atlas or book follows the rules for the bibliographic description of atlases or books. However, it will differ in certain respects, as described below.

3. Special Features

Complete Works

The content of the bibliographic entry is determined mainly by the language(s) of the information appearing in the bibliographic information source(s) and by the language(s) of the bibliography's intended audience. Both these factors should be considered in choosing the language to be used in the entry.

A bilingual document may contain:

1. Two unilingual information sources, presented in tumble or tête-bêche format or arranged continuously;

2. Two bilingual information sources, presented in tumble or tête-bêche format or arranged continuously; or

3. One bilingual information source.

Illustration no. 26   ***SUMMARY OF RULES GOVERNING INFORMATION SOURCES IN BILINGUAL DOCUMENTS***

Information Source	Source our Elements to Use
1. Two unilingual information sources presented in tumble or tête-bêche format or arranged continuously	The information source in the language of the intended audience
2. Two bilingual information sources presented in tumble or tête-bêche format or arranged continuously	The information elements in the language of the intended audience (Exception: titles, which are recorded in their entirety in the title field in the same order given in the information source and are separated by equals signs)
3. One bilingual information source	The information elements in the language of the intended audience (Exception: titles, which are recorded in their entirety in the title field in the same order given in the information source and are separated by equals signs)

The bibliography may be intended for:

1. A unilingual audience or

2. An audience that understands both languages in which the document is written.

For a document containing two unilingual information sources, the entry should be based on the information source that is in the language of the bibliography's intended audience. Therefore, if the intended users are Anglophone, the English-language information source is used.

For a document with one or two bilingual information sources, each listing some or all of the bibliographic information in both languages (e.g., a title page that gives the corporate author name in both languages or a title page verso that cites the publisher's name in both languages), all the information, except the title, should be given in the language of the bibliography's intended audience. All versions of the title should be recorded, separated by equals signs (=) and in the same order as given in the bibliographic information source (see Rule 63.

For documents with separately numbered parts (e.g., text on inverted pages), the number of pages in each part is indicated in the extent field (e.g., 51, 52 p.).

The notes field should provide the following information:

1. the version of the title that is not recorded in the title field; this title is introduced by the expression "Title of additional title-page:"; and

SUMMARY OF RULES GOVERNING INFORMATION SOURCES
IN BILINGUAL DOCUMENT PARTS   *Illustration no. 27*

Type of Information Source	Source or Elements to Use
1. Unilingual information sources for both the part and the host document	The information source in the language of the intended audience
2. Unilingual information sources fort the part and bilingual sources for the host document	The information elements in the language of the intended audience (Exception: titles of the host document, which are recorded in their entirety in the title field in the same order given in the information source and are separated by equals signs)
3. Bilingual information sources for both the part and the host document	The information elements in the language of the intended audience (Exception: the titles, which are recorded in their entirety in the title field in the same order given in the main information source and are

2. the physical features of the format:
   - Text in English and French with French text on inverted pages
   - English and French text in parallel columns
   - English and French text on facing pages

Bilingual Document Part

A bibliographic entry for part of a bilingual document (e.g., a chapter of a book or an article from a periodical) follows the entry outline for a document part (see Rule 4). The entry should provide specific information about the document part (i.e., the author's name and the title of the part) and the information required to identify the host document accurately, according to the guidelines provided above for describing a complete bilingual document. In other words, the factors to be considered in creating the entry are the language(s) of the information appearing in the information source(s) for the document part and for the host document. As stated previously, if each information source is unilingual, the entry should be based on the source that is in the language of the intended users. If the information sources are bilingual, only the bibliographic elements in the language of the intended users are recorded, except for titles, which are entered in their entirety in the title field.

4. *Examples*

For each bilingual document used as an example in this section, there are two entries, one in English and one in French. However, a bibliography certainly need not contain two entries for every bilingual document. The decision to include two entries for a bilingual document will depend on the linguistic knowledge and preference of the intended users. For instance, a bibliography compiled by a federal government department and intended for an audience that knows English and French will contain entries in both languages. However, a bibliography compiled by a private agency for a unilingual audience may contain entries in only one language.

When two different entries are created for one document, they should be cross-referenced, in order to indicate clearly that they refer to the same document and not two different works. If only one entry is created for a bilingual document, the bibliography should list the unused title with a cross-reference to the entry, if there is reason to believe that users may search for the document under its other title.

The examples chosen to illustrate the above conventions consist of English-French documents. However, the same conventions apply to works in other languages or in more than two languages. The examples are listed according to type of information source available (e.g., two unilingual information sources, two bilingual information sources, or one bilingual information source).

Complete Works

1. *Two Unilingual Information Sources*

Tumble Format

Books

Franklin, Karen. – You name it! : helpful hints for editors of Canadian journals, reports, newspapers, and other serial publications. – For the Committee on Bibliography and Information Services for the Social Sciences and Humanities. – Ottawa : National Library of Canada, 1984. – 41, 42 p. – Title of additional title-page: Un titre s'il vous plaît. – Text in English and French with French text on inverted pages. – Cat. no. : SN3-196/1984. – ISBN 0-662-52774-7

Voir la notice correspondante sous

Franklin, Karen. – Un titre s'il vous plaît

Franklin, Karen. – Un titre s'il vous plaît : conseils à l'intention des éditeurs de revues spécialisées, rapports, journaux et autres publications en série canadiennes. – Pour le Comité de la bibliographie et des services d'information en sciences humaines. – Ottawa : Bibliothèque nationale du Canada, 1984. – 42, 41 p. – Titre de la p. de t. additionnelle : You name it!. – Texte en anglais et en français disposé tête-bêche. – No de cat. : SN3-196/1984. – ISBN 0-662-52774-7

See equivalent entry under

Franklin, Karen. -- You name it!

Serials

At the Centre. – Canadian Centre for Occupational Health and Safety. – Vol. 8, no. 1 (March 1985)-   . – Hamilton, Ont. : the Centre, 1985-   .   vol. – Title on additional t.-p.: Au centre. – Text in English and French with French text on inverted pages. – ISSN 0226-9422

Voir la notice correspondante sous

Au Centre

Au Centre. – Centre canadien d'hygiène et de sécurité au travail. – Vol. 8, no. 1 (mars 1985)-   . – Hamilton, Ont. : le Centre, 1985-   .   vol. – Titre de la p. de t. additionelle : At the Centre. – Texte en anglais et en français disposé tête-bêche. – ISSN 0226-9422

See equivalent entry under

At the Centre

Continuous Text

Books

National Library of Canada. – Management manual - personnel. – [Ottawa : s.n., s.d.]. – 2 vol. – Additional title on t.-p.: Guide de gestion du personnel. – Looseleaf format. – Text in English and French

Voir la notice correspondante sous
Bibliothèque nationale du Canada. – Guide de gestion du personnel

Bibliothèque nationale du Canada. – Guide de gestion du personnel. – [Ottawa : s.n., s.d.]. – 2 vol. – Titre additionnel de la p. de t. : Management manual - personnel. – Texte en anglais et en français

See equivalent entry under

National Library of Canada. – Management manual - personnel

Serials

The Canadian composer. – Composers, Authors and Publishers Association of Canada. – No. 54 (November 1970)-   . – Toronto : Creative Arts, 1970-   . – vol. – Title of additional t.-p.: Le compositeur canadien. – Text in English and French. – ISSN 0008-3259

Voir la notice correspondante sous
Le compositeur canadien

Le compositeur canadien. – Association des compositeurs, auteurs et éditeurs du Canada. – N° 54 (nov. 1970)-   . – Toronto : Creative Arts, 1970-   . – vol. – Titre de la p. de t. additionelle : The Canadian composer. – Texte en anglais et en français. – ISSN 0008-3259

See equivalent entry under
The Canadian composer

2. Two Bilingual Information Sources

Tumble Format

Books

In the example below, the name of the corporate author (which is also the publisher) is given in both languages on each of the two title pages. However, in the entries, the name is given only in the language of the intended audience.

> Canadian Broadcasting Corporation. – Culture, broadcasting, and the Canadian Identity : a submission to the Cultural Policy Review Committee. – [Ottawa] : the Corporation, 1981. – 27, 27 p. – Title of additional title-page : Culture, radiodiffusion et identité canadienne : mémoire présenté au Comité d'étude de la politique culturelle. – Text in English and French with French text on inverted pages

> **Voir la notice correspondante sous**
> **Société Radio-Canada. – Culture, radiodiffusion et identité canadienne**

> Société Radio-Canada. – Culture, radiodiffusion et identité canadienne : mémoire présenté au Comité d'étude de la politique culturelle. – [Ottawa] : la Société, 1981. – 27, 27 p. – Titre de la p. de t. additionnelle : Culture, broadcasting, and the Canadian identity : a submission to the Cultural Policy Review Committee. – Texte en français et en anglais disposé tête-bêche

> **See equivalent entry under**
> **Canadian Broadcasting Corporation. – Culture, broadcasting, and the Canadian identity**

Serials

In the example below, the title of the serial publication is given in both languages on each of the title pages. Consequently, both versions of the title are entered in the title field, in accordance with Number 3 ("Special Features") at the beginning of this chapter.

> Newsletter = Bulletin . – Associate Committee on Instructional Technology, National Research Council of Canada. – No. 11 (1981)-   . – Ottawa : the Council, 1981-   . –   vol. – Text in English and French with French text on inverted pages. – ISSN 0700-1606

> Newsletter = Bulletin . – Comité associé de technologie pédagogique, Conseil national de recherches du Canada. – No 11 (1981)-   . – Ottawa : le Conseil, 1981-   . –   vol. – Texte en anglais et en français disposé tête-bêche. – ISSN 0700-1606

In the above example, the English title is listed before the French title in the document. The bibliography should therefore contain a cross-reference under the publication's French title. This cross-reference cites the English title, followed by an equals sign and the French title.

Bulletin. – Comité associé de technologie pédagogique

> VOIR

Newsletter = Bulletin. – Comité associé de technologie pédagogique

3. One Bilingual Information Source

Books

Evans, Gwynneth. – Women in federal politics : a bio-bibliography = Les femmes au fédéral : une bio-bibliographie. – Editor, Marion C. Wilson. – Ottawa : National Library of Canada, 1975. – Text in English and French

Evans, Gwynneth. – Women in federal politics : a bio-bibliography = Les femmes au fédéral : une bio-bibliographie. – Éditeur, Marion C. Wilson. – Ottawa : Bibliothèque nationale du Canada, 1975. – Texte en anglais et en français

The document used as an example above lists the English title before the French title. The bibliography should therefore contain a cross-reference under the publication's French title. This cross-reference cites the English title, followed by an equals sign and the French title.

Evans, Gwynneth. – Les femmes au fédéral : une bio-bibliographie.

> VOIR

Evans, Gwynneth. – Women in federal politics : a bio-bibliography = Les femmes au fédéral : une bio-bibliographie.

Serials

University affairs = Affaires universitaires. – Association of Universities and Colleges of Canada. – Vol. 1 (1959)-   . – Ottawa : AUCC, 1959. –   vol. – Text in English and French. – ISSN 0041-9527

University affairs = Affaires universitaires. – Association des Universités et Collèges du Canada. – Vol 1 (1959)-   . – Ottawa : AUCC, 1959. –   vol. – Texte en anglais et en français. – ISSN 0041-9527

The serial publication used as an example above lists the English title before the French title. The bibliography therefore contains a cross-reference under the French title. This cross-reference cites the English title, followed by an equals sign and the French title.

Affaires universitaires. – Association des Universités et Collèges du Canada

> VOIR

University affairs = Affaires universitaires. – Association des Universités et Collèges du Canada

Sound Recordings

Berlioz, Hector. – Harold en Italie [sound recording] = Harold in Italy. – Orchestre symphonique de Québec, Simon Streatfield, conductor. – Toronto : CBC Enterprises, p1985. – 1 audiocassette. – Edition no. CBC Enterprises SMC 5047

Berlioz, Hector. – Harold en Italie [enregistrement sonore] = Harold in Italy. – Orchestre symphonique de Québec, Simon Streatfield, chef d'orchestre. – Toronto : Entreprises Radio-Canada, p1985. – 1 audiocasette. – No d'éd.: Entreprises Radio-Canada, SMC 5047

Berlioz, Hector. – Harold in Italy

> SEE

Berlioz, Hector. – Harold en Italie [enregistrement sonore] = Harold in Italy

Atlases

Dudycha, Douglas J., et al. – The Canadian atlas of recreation and exercise = L'atlas canadien de la récréation et de l'activité physique. – Waterloo, Ont. : Dept. of Geography, University of Waterloo, 1983. – 1 atlas. – (Department of Geography Publication Series ; no. 21). – English and French text in parallel columns

Dudycha, Douglas J. et al. – The Canadian atlas of recreation and exercise = L'atlas canadien de la récréation et de l'activité physique. – Waterloo, Ont. : Dept. of Geography, University of Waterloo, 1983. – 1 atlas. – (Série de publications du Département de géographie ; no 21). – Texte en anglais et en français sur des col. parallèles

Dudycha, Douglas J. et al. – L'atlas canadien de la récréation et de l'activité physique

> VOIR

Dudycha, Douglas J. et al. – The Canadian atlas of recreation and exercise = L'atlas canadien de la récréation et de l'activité physique

Microforms

Gazetteer of Canada. British Columbia [microform] = Répertoire géographique du Canada. Colombie-Britannique. – [Ottawa : Surveys and Mapping Branch], 1985. – 6 microfiches. – Text in English and French. – Reproduction of 3rd ed.

Gazetteer of Canada. British Columbia [microforme] = Répertoire géographique du Canada. Colombie-Britannique. – [Ottawa : Direction des levés et de la cartographie], 1985. – 6 microfiches. – Texte en anglais et en français. – Reproduction de la 3e éd.

Répertoire géographique du Canada. Colombie-Britannique

> VOIR

Gazetteer of Canada. British Columbia [microform] = Répertoire géographique du Canada. Colombie-Britannique

Bilingual Document Part

1. Unilingual Information Source for Both the Document Part and the Host Document

Tumble Format

Book Parts

Eichler, Margrit ; Lapointe, Jeanne. – «A dual perspective in social science and humanities research». – On the treatment of the sexes in research. – Ottawa : Social Sciences and Humanities Research Council of Canada, c1985. – Title of additional title-page: Le traitement objectif des sexes dans la recherche. – Text in English and French with French text on inverted pages. – Cat. no. CR22-22/1985. – ISBN 0-662-53610-X. – P. 19-22

Voir la notice correspondante sous
Lapointe, Jeanne ; Eichler, Margrit. – «Avantages de la dualité de perspective pour la recherche en sciences humaines»

Lapointe, Jeanne ; Eichler, Margrit. – «Avantages de la dualité de perspective pour la recherche en sciences humaines». – Le traitement objectif des sexes dans la recherche. – Ottawa : Conseil de recherches en sciences humaines du Canada, c1985. – Titre de la p. de t. additionnelle : On the treatment of the sexes in research. – Texte en anglais et en français disposé tête-bêche. – No de cat. : CR22-22/1985. – ISBN 0-662-53610-X. – P. 21-25

See equivalent entry under
Eichler, Margrit ; Lapointe, Jeanne. – «A dual perspective in science and humanities research»

In the example above, the authors' names are inverted in the document.

Serials

Pérusse, Michel. – «Behaviour in the face of danger». – At the Centre. – Canadian Centre for Occupational Health and Safety. – Vol. 8, no. 1 (Mar. 1985). – Title on additional t.-p.: Au Centre. – Text in English and French with French text on inverted pages. – ISSN 0226-9422. – P. 5-6

Voir la notice correspondante sous
Pérusse, Michel. – «Le comportement face aux dangers»

Pérusse, Michel. – «Le comportement face aux dangers». – Au Centre. – Centre Canadien d'hygiène et de sécurité au travail. Vol. 8, n° 1 (mars 1985). – Titre de la p. de t. additionelle : At the Centre. – Texte anglais et français disposé tête-bêche. – ISSN 0226-9422. – P. 5-6

See equivalent entry under
Pérusse, Michel. -- «Behaviour in the face of danger»

Continuous Text

Books

National Library of Canada. – «Staff relations». – Management manual - personnel. – [Ottawa : s.n., s.d.]. – Additional title on t.-p.: Guide de gestion du personnel. – Looseleaf format. – Text in English and French. – Ch. 3

Voir la notice correspondante sous
Bibliothèque nationale du Canada. – «Relations de travail»

Bibliothèque nationale du Canada. – «Relations de travail». – Guide de gestion du personnel. – [Ottawa : s.n., s.d.]. – Titre additionnel de la p. de t. : Management manual - personnel. – Texte en anglais et en français. – Ch. 3

See equivalent entry under
National Library of Canada. – «Staff relations»

Serials

Moore, Mavor. – «Who's got the money and how can we get our hands on it?». – The Canadian composer. – Composers, Authors and Publishers Association of Canada. – No. 54 (Nov. 1970). – Added title-page title : Le compositeur canadien. – Text in English and French. – ISSN 0008-3259. – P. 18,20

Voir la notice correspondante sous
Moore, Mavor. – «Qui a l'argent et comment mettre la main dessus?»

Moore, Mavor. – «Qui a l'argent et comment mettre la main dessus?». – Le compositeur canadien. – Association des compositeurs, auteurs et éditeurs du Canada. – No 54 (nov. 1970). – Titre de la p. de t. additionnelle : The Canadian composer. – Texte en anglais et en français. – ISSN 0008-3259. – P. 19,21

See equivalent entry under
Moore, Mavor. – «Who's got the money and how can we get our hands on It?»

2. Unilingual Information Source for the Document Part and Bilingual Information Source for the Host Document

Tumble Format

Books

Canadian Broadcasting Corporation. – «The Canadian broadcasting system : an objective unfulfilled». – Culture, broadcasting, and the Canadian identity : a submission to the Cultural Policy Review Committee. – [Ottawa] : the Corporation, 1981. – Title of additional title-page: Culture, radiodiffusion et identité canadienne : mémoire présenté au Comité d'étude de la politique culturelle. – Text in English and French with French on inverted pages. – P. 9-11

Voir la notice correspondante sous
Société Radio-Canada. – «Le système de la radiodiffusion canadienne : un objectif qui n'est pas atteint»

Société Radio-Canada. – «Le système de la radiodiffusion canadienne : un objectif qui n'est pas atteint». – Culture, radiodiffusion et identité canadienne : mémoire présenté au Comité d'étude de la politique culturelle. – [Ottawa] : la

Société, 1981. – Titre de la p. de t. additionnelle : Culture, broadcasting, and the Canadian identity : a submission to the Cultural Policy Review Committee. – Texte en français et en anglais disposé tête-bêche. – P. 9-11

See equivalent entry under
Canadian Broadcasting Corporation. – «The Canadian broadcasting system : an objective unfulfilled»

Serials

Arnold, W.A. – «Impressions of art education in Ontario». – Canadian studies bulletin = Bulletin des études canadiennes. – Association of Canadian Community Colleges. – (Sept./Oct. 1986). – Text in English and French with French text on inverted pages. – P. 7, 11, 13

Voir la notice correspondante sous
Arnold, W.A. – «Enseignement des arts en Ontario»

Arnold, W.A. – «Enseignement des arts en Ontario». – Canadian studies bulletin = Bulletin des études canadiennes. – Association des Collèges communautaires du Canada. – (Sept./oct. 1986). – Texte en anglais et en français disposé tête-bêche. – P. 5, 9, 17

See equivalent entry under
Arnold, W.A. – «Impressions of art education in Ontario»

Continuous Text

Books

Evans, Gwynneth. – «Albanie (Paré) Morin 1921- ». – Women in federal politics : a bio-bibliography = Les femmes au fédéral : une bio-bibliographie. – Editor, Marion C. Wilson. – Ottawa : National Library of Canada, 1975. – English and French texts in parallel columns. – P. 61-62

Evans, Gwynneth. – «Albanie (Paré) Morin 1921- ». – Women in federal politics : a bio-bibliography = Les femmes au fédéral : une bio-bibliographie. – Editeur, Marion C. Wilson. – Ottawa : Bibliothèque nationale du Canada, 1975. – Texte en anglais et en français sur des col. parallèles. – P. 62

Serials

Pierre, Gloria. – «Climate oppressive in B.C.». – University affairs = Affaires universitaires. – Association of Universities and Colleges of Canada. – Vol. 26, no. 5 (May 1985). – Text in English and French. – ISSN 0041-9257. – P. 2

Voir la notice correspondante sous
Pierre, Gloria. – «Climat oppresif en C.-B.»

Pierre, Gloria. – «Climat oppressif en C.-B.». –University affairs = Affaires universitaires. – Association des Universités et Collèges du Canada. – Vol. 26, no 5 (mai 1985). – Texte en anglais et en français. – ISSN 0041-9257. – P. 3

See equivalent entry under
Pierre, Gloria. – «Climate oppresive in B.C.»

3. Bilingual Information Source for Both the Document Part and the Host Document

Thorngate, Warren ; Ferguson, Tamara. – «Behind the eyeball : some popular misuses of information in human decision making = Au-delà des apparences : quelques mésusages courants de l'information dans des décisions humaines». – The Canadian journal of information science = Revue canadienne des sciences de l'information. – Vol. 2, no. 1 (May 1977). – ISSN 0380-9218. – P. 1-11

Thorngate, Warren ; Ferguson, Tamara. – «Behind the eyeball : some popular misuses of information in human decision making = Au-delà des apparences : quelques mésusages courants de l'information dans des décisions humaines». – The Canadian journal of information science = Revue canadienne des sciences de l'information. – Vol. 2, n° 1 (mai 1977). – Résumé en anglais et en français, texte en anglais seulement. – ISSN 0380-9218. – P. 1-11

The serial part used as an example above gives the English title before the French title. The bibliography should therefore contain a cross-reference under the French title of the publication. This cross-reference cites the English title of the document, followed by an equals sign and the French title.

Thorngate, Warren ; Ferguson, Tamara. «Au-delà des apparences : quelques mésusages courants de l'information dans des décisions humaines»

VOIR

Thorngate, Warren ; Ferguson, Tamara. – «Behind the eyeball : some popular misuses of information in human decision making = Au-delà des apparences : quelques mésusages courants de l'information dans des décisions humaines»

Appendix

Below is a list of terms often found in bibliographies, with their abbreviations or usually substituted Latin forms. The Latin terms or expressions are not underlined or italicized. Words that are not shortened forms are not followed by periods.

abbreviation	abbr.
adaptation	adapt.
and other people	et al.
and other things, and so forth	etc.
appendix	app.
augmented	augm.
bibliography	bibliogr.
biography	biog.
black and white	b&w
book	b.
bulletin	bull.
chapter	ch.
collection	coll.
column	col.
compiled	comp.
corrected	corr.
colour	col.
copyright	©
edition	ed.
et alii	et al.
(and other people)	
et cetera	etc.
(and other things, and so forth)	
exempli gratia	e.g.
(for example)	
facsimile	facsim.
figure	fig.
folio	fol.

for example	e.g.
hardbound	hb.
id est	i.e.
(that is)	
illustration	ill.
introduction	introd.
(by)	
new series	new ser.
number	no.
page	p.
paperbound	pb.
paragraph	par.
part	pt.
plate	pl.
preface	pref.
pseudonym	pseud.
reprint	repr.
revised	rev.
section	sec.
series	ser.
sheet	sht.
sine die	s.d.
(without date)	
sine loco	s.l.
(without place)	
sine nomine	s.n.
(without name)	
supplement	suppl.
table	tab.
that is	i.e.
thus	sic
title-page	t.-p.
translated	trans.
versus	v.
volume	vol.
without date	s.d.
(sine date)	
without place	s.l.
(sine loco)	
without name	s.n.
(sine nomine)	

Bibliography

Abbreviations : a Canadian handbook. – Ed. T. Dobroslavic, S. Yates. – Vancouver : First Avenue Press, 1985. – 173 p. – ISBN 0-920557-00-7

Abbreviations dictionary. – Comp. Ralph De Sola. – Expanded international 6th ed. – New York : Elsevier, c1981. – 966 p. – ISBN 0-444-00380-0

Acronyms, initialisms & abbreviations dictionary : a guide to more than 450 000 acronyms, initialisms, abbreviations, contractions, alphabetic symbols, and similar condensed apellations. – Ed. Julie E. Towell. – 13th ed. – Detroit : Gale Research, c1989. – 3 vols. – ISBN 0-8103-2581-0

American National Standards Institute. – American national standard for information sciences : abbreviation of titles of publications. – New York : the Institute, 1985. – 12 p. – Reference no. ANSI Z39.5-1985. – ISSN 8756-0860

The Canadian style: a guide to writing and editing. – Toronto: Dundur Press, 1985. – 256 p. – ISBN 0-919670-93-8

International Federation of Library Associations and Institutions. – ISBD(G) : General international standard bibliographic description : annotated text. – Prepared by the Working Group on the General International Standard Bibliographic Description set up by the IFLA Committee on Cataloguing. – London : IFLA International Office for UBC, 1977. – 24 p. – ISBN 0903043181

International Federation of Library Association = and Institutions. – ISBD(G) : General international standard bibliographic description : annotated text. – Prepared by the Working Group on the General International Standard Bibliographic Description set up by the IFLA Committee on Cataloguing. – London : IFLA International Office for UBC, 1977. – 24 p. – ISBN 0-903043-16-1

International Organization for Standardization. – Documentation, bibliographic references, abbreviations of typical words = Documentation, références bibliographiques, abréviations des mots typiques. – [Geneva] : the Organization, c1975. – 38 p. – Reference no. ISO 832-1975 (E/F)

International Organization for Standardization. – Documentation, bibliographic references, content, form and structure. – 2nd ed. – [Geneva] : the Organization, c1987. 11 p. – Reference no. ISO 690:1987(E). – French title: Documentation, références bibliographiques : contenu, forme et structure

International Organization for Standardization. – Documentation, romanization of Chinese. – 1st ed. – [Geneva] : the Organization, c1982. – 5 p. – Reference no. ISO 7098-1982(E). – French title: Documentation, romanisation du chinois

International Organization for Standardization. – Documentation, rules for the abbreviation of title words and titles of publications. – 2nd ed. – [Geneva] : the Organization, c1984. – 5 p. – Reference no. ISO 4-1984(E). – French title: Documentation, règles pour l'abréviation des mots dans les titres et des titres de publication

International Organization for Standardization. – Documentation, transliteration of Arabic characters into Latin characters. – 1st ed. – [Geneva] : the Organization, c1984. – 7 p. – Reference no. ISO 233-1984(E). – French title: Documentation, translittération des caractères arabes en caractères latins

International Organization for Standardization. – Documentation, transliteration of Hebrew characters into Latin characters. – 1st ed. – [Geneva] : the Organization, c1984. – 8 p. – Reference no. ISO 259-1984(E). – French title: Documentation, translittération des caractères hébraiques en caractères latins

International Organization for Standardization. – Documentation, transliteration of Slavic Cyrillic characters into Latin characters. – 1st ed. – [Geneva] : the Organization, c1986. – 8 p. – Reference no. ISO 9-1986(E). – French title: Documentation, translittération des caractères cyrilliques slaves en caractères latins

Joint Steering Committee for Revision of AACR. – Anglo-American cataloguing rules. – Ed. Michael Gorman, Paul W. Winkler. – 2nd ed., 1988 revision. – Ottawa : Canadian Library Association, c1988. – 677 p. – ISBN 0-88802-242-5

Library of Congress. Processing Services. – Cataloging service bulletin. – No. 1 (Summer 1978)-   . – Washington : the Services, 1978-   . –   vol. – ISSN 0160-8029

Reverse acronyms, initialisms & abbreviations dictionary. – Ed. Julie E. Towell and Helen E. Sheppard. – 10th ed. – Detroit : Gale Research, 1985. – 3 vol. – ISBN 0-8103-0684-0

Index

When present, numbers in brackets refer to rule no.